_Kw_

Wiltshire
College
Lackham

Lacock
Chippenham
Wiltshire
SN15 2NY

D0539538

ECONOMICS OF WOODLAND MANAGEMENT

Applied Ecology and Natural Resource Management Series
B. Hackett, *Landscape Conservation*
D. R. Helliwell, *Options in Forestry*
(others in preparation)

ECONOMICS OF
WOODLAND MANAGEMENT

D. R. Helliwell
BSc(forestry), MSc, DipLA, FICFor, MIBiol, FArborA

PACKARD PUBLISHING LIMITED
CHICHESTER

© 1984 D. R. Helliwell

First published in 1984
by Packard Publishing Limited, 16 Lynch Down,
Funtington, Chichester, West Sussex PO18 9LR

British Library Cataloguing in Publication Data
Helliwell, Denis Rodney
    Economics of woodland management.
    1. Forest conservation—Great Britain
    2. Forest management—Great Britain
    I. Title
    333.75'0941   SD414.G7

    ISBN 0-906527-07-4 (pbk only)

Typeset by Pauline Newton, Chichester, West Sussex
Cover and layout by Bruce Williams Designs, Chichester, West Sussex
Printed in the United Kingdom by Olivers Printing Works Limited,
Battle, East Sussex

CONTENTS

		Page
Preface		viii
Introduction		1
1.	Photosynthesis, energy, and labour	1
2.	Land and climate	5
3.	Capital investment, time-preference, and discount rates	7
4.	Costs	9
	a) Land	9
	b) Supervision and labour	10
5.	Silvicultural systems	12
6.	Timber production	17
	a) Size of enterprise	17
	b) Size and distribution of individual stands	18
	c) Harvesting methods	19
	d) Timber prices	21
7.	Nature conservation	23
	a) Size and distribution of woodlands	23
	b) Tree species	23
	c) Silvicultural systems and methods	24
	d) Valuation of benefits	25
8.	Amenity and recreation	26
	a) Size and distribution of woodlands	27
	b) Tree species	27
	c) Silvicultural systems	28
	d) Valuation of benefits	28
9.	Forestry and other land uses	29
	a) Water supplies	29
	b) Farming	30
	c) Hunting and shooting	31
	d) Fishing	32
10.	Tree species and timber production	32
	a) Volume and value	32
	b) Markets and prices	33
	c) Windthrow	34
	d) Pests and diseases	35

Contents continued . . .

11. **Forestry practice**.............................. 36
     a) Ploughing and draining 36
     b) Plants and planting 36
     c) Weeding and cleaning 37
     d) Brashing and pruning......................... 38
     e) Thinning.................................... 39
     f) Felling and extraction of timber 41
     g) Fencing and pest control...................... 41
     h) Forest roads 44
     i) Fire precautions 45
     j) Yield control and timber measurement.......... 46
12. **Ownership and management**...................... 47
     a) Types of woodland ownership.................. 47
     b) Foresters, agents, consultants, and contractors 48
     c) Woodland accounts........................... 49
     d) Cash flow 50
     e) Grants and taxes 51
13. **The future demand for woodland products**.......... 52
     Useful books and papers....................... 54
     Useful addresses 55
     Glossary 56
     **Appendix 1: Valuation of woodlands for amenity
          purposes**.................................. 57
     **Appendix 2: Some typical costs and benefits of
          managing woodlands of different types; sizes
          of woodland – 1 ha, 10 ha, 100 ha, 1000 ha** 59

List of Figures

1. Silvicultural systems 13
2. Clear felling system 14
3. Shelterwood system 14
4. Group selection system 14
5. Selection system................................ 14
6. A comparison of the numbers of trees of different sizes
   removed under clear-felling and selection systems ... 16
7. Relationships between various aspects of the environment and its visual attractiveness 29
8. Costs of felling and removing timber from even-aged
   crops 40

List of Tables

1. Comparative production of crops 3
2. Ratio of energy gained and energy used in producing various crops 3
3. Productivity of major site types (m³ per hectare per year) 6
4. Typical values of land and crops (£ per hectare 1982) ... 10
5. Comparative costs of felling, extracting, and loading timber on a woodland estate of 10 000 ha in areas of different size and distribution 19
6. Typical costs (£) of producing timber products (1982) .. 21
7. Typical prices of standing oak timber of different size and quality (£/m³ in 1982) 22
8. Typical prices of standing spruce timber of different sizes (£/m³ in 1982) 22
9. Value of different tree species for nature conservation ... 24
10. Comparative annual volume production and value of different tree species on different sites (1981 prices) .. 33
11. Typical markets and standing prices for various sizes and types of timber (£/m³, 1981) 34
12. Approximate costs of planting, expressed in man-hour equivalents per hectare (1982 prices) 37
13. Approximate costs of weeding (man-hour equivalents per hectare) 37
14. Typical costs of brashing and pruning 39
15. Approximate costs (in man-hour equivalents per hectare per year) of maintaining fences around square woodland areas of different sizes 42
16. Typical net costs of pest control in forest areas of 500 ha or more (man-hours/ha/year) 43
17. Typical costs of forest roads (£/km, 1981 prices) 44
18. Approximate costs of marking, measuring, and selling timber (man-hours/ha/year, 1982 prices) 47

PREFACE

At the time of writing there appears to be no book which attempts to explain the economics of woodland management in a way which is relevant to those with a non-professional interest in forestry, such as farmers, naturalists, parish councillors, ramblers, or potential woodland investors. There also appears to be a need for a book which could be useful to those actually engaged in forestry, by setting out the various factors at work in general terms, rather than concentrating on the details of current costs and prices or the details of particular crops or silvicultural methods.

In dealing with the economics of woodland management it has been necessary to describe very briefly the various methods and practices involved, but no attempt has been made to provide a guide to forestry practice as such. For this, the reader is referred elsewhere.

D.R.H.

December 1982

INTRODUCTION

Many different factors can affect the economics of woodland management, and several of these can operate at any one time, giving a very wide range of possible results. Each woodland, and each stand of trees within a woodland, tends to differ in some respects from every other, making it impossible to give simple answers to questions such as How much is a mature ash tree worth? or What sort of trees should I plant on my farm? The different factors which are involved form the subject matter of this book, but it must be constantly borne in mind that none of these is completely unrelated in its effect. For example, one particular 10-hectare woodland may be highly profitable, due to a particular combination of easy access, good soil, careful husbandry, and proximity to a sawmill, whereas another woodland of similar size but with poorer access, different tree species, or less competent or efficient management may show a net loss.

The factors which are of most relevance in this context are likely to be:

    i. the size of the woodland;
    ii. the size of the woodland enterprise;
    iii. the quality of the site in terms of soil and climate (and hence the quality and size of the timber produced);
    iv. ease of access for removal of timber;
    v. proximity to markets for timber;
    vi. the value placed on wildlife and amenity;
    vii. the need, if any, to fence against rabbits, deer, sheep, and so on;
    viii. the incidence of taxes and tax allowances;
    ix. the quality of present and past management.

These factors are covered in the following chapters, although not in exactly the same order.

1. PHOTOSYNTHESIS, ENERGY, AND LABOUR

Photosynthesis is the process whereby green plants use sunlight to convert water and carbon dioxide into carbohydrates. This process has a maximum theoretical efficiency of about thirty-three per cent. As plants are rarely completely efficient, this figure is unlikely to be obtained in practice; and, as all the various wavelengths of sunlight are not equally effective, only about eleven per cent of the total incoming solar radiation is likely to be converted into stored energy. Even this is an over-estimate, as the plant uses some energy in its internal processes, and some light is lost through reflection or transmission through the leaves. Therefore the most that is likely to be converted into carbohydrates and other materials stored in the plant is about five per cent of the incoming radiation. Under most agricultural and forestry systems the figure is likely to be much less than this, for several reasons:

i.   the crop does not always cover the ground completely;
ii.   there may be insufficient moisture, aeration, or nutrient supply in the soil;
iii. air and soil temperatures may be too high or too low for maximum efficiency;
iv.   pests, disease or physical damage may reduce yields;
v.   there may be insufficient carbon dioxide for maximum production, especially on windless days during active photosynthesis;
vi.   only a proportion of the total annual production is harvested.

   In the British Isles, a five per cent conversion of solar radiation would give a yield of about 88 tonnes of dry matter per hectare per year. In practice, maximum harvested yields rarely exceed one quarter of this, representing a conversion of only one and a quarter per cent of incoming solar radiation. Even in a fully stocked forest on a productive site for example, much of the annual production goes into leaves, twigs, and roots, which are not normally harvested. (If they were harvested, there might be problems in maintaining soil fertility, and other problems, which make it less attractive than it might seem at first sight.) In agricultural crops there are also parts of the plant which are not harvested (e.g., the roots of cereals, and the finer roots and the leaves of sugar beet) and there is usually a period when the crop covers only part of the ground. The *maximum feasible* production of harvestable dry matter under open-field conditions in the British Isles is therefore not more than about 22 tonnes/hectare/year, under agriculture or forestry.

   Needless to say, *average* yields are much less than this, at about 7 dry tonnes per hectare on good land. This equals about 29 tonnes, fresh weight of potatoes, 20 tonnes of softwood timber, or 13 tonnes of hardwood timber.

   Table 1 gives a comparison of the harvestable dry matter production of three typical crops under British conditions.

Table 1 — Comparative production of crops

| | | (tonnes per hectare per year) | | |
		Oak	Spruce	Potatoes
Average	Fresh weight	6	14	30
	Dry weight	3.25	4.75	6.5
	Net gain*	3	4.25	2.75
Feasible maximum	Fresh weight	10	30	88
	Dry weight	5.25	10	19
	Net gain**	4.75	9	8

* The figure for average Net gain assumes typical inputs of fertilizer, herbicides, and harvesting machinery, and refers to the energy used to grow and move the product to the farm or forest gate. Energy used to produce sawn oak, paper products, or potato crisps is not included, nor is delivery to the customer.
** The figure for feasible maximum Net gain assumes that energy inputs rise in direct proportion to output, which may or may not be true in any particular case.

The figures for Net gain given in Table 1 are based on current practice, and it is interesting to note the amount of energy which is used, in the form of petroleum, electricity, manufactured chemicals, and animal feedstuff, in the production of various crops (Table 2).

Table 2 — Ratio of energy gained and energy used in producing various crops

	Energy produced	Energy used
Battery poultry (meat)	1	9
Battery eggs	1	6
Intensive beef	1	6
Milk	1	2
Mutton	1	2
Ocean fisheries	1	2
Potatoes	1	0.5
Wheat	1	0.3
Timber	1	0.1

This obviously shows timber production in a very favourable light, but it must be added that many timber products, such as hardboard, chipboard, and paper pulp, require a considerable further input of energy during manufacture and distribution. But, equally, much of the food which is sold in shops has also had a large input of energy in transport, processing, and packaging. On the other hand, some timber is used in the round with little further expenditure of energy, or after sawing and seasoning at a local mill which uses only a small amount of energy, often supplied by combustion of waste wood.

The amount of labour involved in producing timber is roughly comparable to that involved in producing the same dry weight of crops in agriculture, requiring about one person per 60 hectares, producing some 300 tonnes of dry matter per year. The exact figure will of course vary, according to the particular crop and method of management. It will also depend on whether or not timber fellers, mechanics, lorry drivers, and others are included in the calculation. It is often said that for every man employed in the woods, seven are employed elsewhere in servicing machinery, and in handling, processing, and marketing the finished product. The same is also true of agriculture, and in both branches of husbandry there has been a consistent trend towards fewer people being employed on the land and proportionally more in associated activities. Whether this trend can continue much further is uncertain, and there may even be some slight reversal of the trend if the price of energy and raw materials increases at a greater rate than the price of labour.

The amount of work which one healthy worker can achieve in a 40-hour week is about the same as can be achieved by the use of one gallon (4.5 litres) of petrol in an efficient piece of machinery. There is therefore no immediate likelihood of manpower replacing the chainsaw, tractor-mounted winch, or other items of machinery. However, the use of ever larger and heavier tractors (costing more per hour than the operator in many cases) may have reached or passed its peak.

Forestry work, like other land-based industries, has traditionally been poorly paid. Many people find it attractive, but as they can usually earn more, and with less effort, by working in a factory, it does not offer a very promising career to those with a family to support. Accordingly, there is a tendency for school-leavers to enter forestry, only to leave a few years later when their financial commitments increase, sometimes returning after an interval of 20 years or more, either as direct employees or as self-employed contractors. The latter can sometimes earn more than direct employees, but this is often more of an illusion than a reality, when the cost of vehicles and other machinery is taken into account. It does, however, offer an interesting and rewarding way of life.

Modern forestry work covers a wide range of skills. Workers should, for example, be able to recognize all the common tree species in summer or in winter (which sounds obvious enough, but can not always be taken for granted, especially if casual labour or farm labour is employed); they may be required to apply herbicides by one of several methods, use a chainsaw efficiently and safely, or operate a four-wheel-drive tractor with one or more winches. The advent of herbicides, chainsaws, and forestry tractors over the past 20 years has done much to increase efficiency in forestry and to make it possible to pay higher wages, but these still tend to lag behind other industries in the British Isles.

2. LAND AND CLIMATE

In a landscape which has been predominantly agricultural for several centuries, woodlands and forests in Britain have usually occupied land which is least suited to farming: areas which are steep or inaccessible, wet or liable to flooding, or where the soil is intractable or infertile. There are of course some woodlands on better sites, which have been managed for amenity, sport, or other reasons, where tree growth is good and it is possible to remove timber without much difficulty. The range of different sites occupied by woodlands is therefore very great, and the type of tree, the rate of growth, and the economics of management vary accordingly.

Land and climate are very closely linked, and the basic conditions for plant growth depend on a combination of the following variables:

> rainfall,
> solar radiation,
> temperature,
> windspeed,
> physical structure of the soil,
> chemical composition of the soil,
> ground slope.

Thus, at a given ground slope, the conditions for tree growth will vary with location and elevation (which will be related to windspeed, temperature, and rainfall) and with the underlying soil type, which will vary according to the basic geology, history of glaciation, climate, and recent land use.

There are interactions between several of these variables, making each dependent to some extent on others. For example, the occurrence of deep peat soils depends on a combination of high rainfall, gentle slope, impeded drainage, and/or low available soil nutrient levels; any two of these factors combined being likely to lead to the formation of peat.

Table 3 covers the major variations in four of the most important variables, indicating typical productivity in terms of timber volume, using current forestry practice and the most productive species for each site.

Table 3 — Productivity of major site types
(m^3 per hectare per year*)

	Soil type			
	Calcareous	Sandy	Clayey	Deep peat**
Low rainfall (< 900 mm)				
Low windspeed. Low elevation	8	10	12	·
High elevation	·	·	·	·
High windspeed. Low elevation	·	·	·	·
High elevation	·	·	·	·
Medium rainfall (900–1500 mm)				
Low windspeed. Low elevation	10	14	18	16
High elevation	8	12	16	14
High windspeed. Low elevation	8	12	14†	14
High elevation	·	·	·	·
High rainfall (> 1500 mm)				
Low windspeed. Low elevation	·	·	·	·
High elevation	10	16	20	16
High windspeed. Low elevation	·	·	·	·
High elevation	8	14	14†	12†

*   1 m^3 is approximately 1 tonne, fresh weight.
**   includes only acid (oligotrophic) peats, and not fen peats.
·   this combination of variables rarely, or never, occurs in the British Isles.
†   tree growth is fairly rapid on such sites, but the trees are likely to be blown down before they reach a very large size. Initial growth rates indicating yields of over 20 m^3/ha/yr are not uncommon, but actual yields are usually less.

The nature of the terrain also influences the ease with which timber can be taken out of the woodland and transported to the mill or factory. Well-drained land with only gentle slopes gives easier conditions than very steep ground or poorly-drained land.

3. CAPITAL INVESTMENT, TIME-PREFERENCE, AND DISCOUNT RATES

The conventional view of investment is that money invested in an enterprise should retain its capital value and also yield a return on an annual or periodic basis. This return, or 'interest', is regarded as payment for having loaned the money rather than having spent it immediately. This view was realistic in a period of rapid techno- logical innovation and plenteous supplies of cheap energy and raw materials. In that period, which broadly encompassed what is known as the Industrial Revolution, there was a premium on capital, which could be almost guaranteed to enable the user to employ more efficient methods of operation than had been used in the past.

We have now moved into a period when the costs of energy and raw materials are rising as quickly as technical skills are developed to make savings with new materials or methods. We may even have passed the point when energy and raw materials increase in price more rapidly than the rate at which technology can compensate for it.

Although it may have been logical to expect investments to grow in value (over and above any effects of 'inflation') in past decades, there is less logic in this assumption at the present time. In fact, in recent years, very many investments have scarcely maintained their value in the face of inflation, and investments which are fairly certain to hold their real value are much sought after. It has therefore become more rewarding to invest in goods such as postage stamps, jewellery, or antique furniture than in manufacturing industry.

Following the conventional view of the last century or so, one could argue that almost all forms of forestry were poor invest- ments. Due to the long time-scale involved in growing trees, it was seen to be better to invest money in almost anything else, because the interest obtained on the capital investment would then be higher. If one had a woodland full of growing timber it would have been most economic to fell it and sell the timber, and then to leave the ground unplanted. Most economic calculations in recent years (and even at the time of writing) have been based on these outmoded assumptions, although there is now a greater realization in some quarters that different economic criteria should be applied, which do not automatically penalize long-term investments such as forestry. There has in fact been a fairly strong market recently

for investments in agricultural land and forestry. These investments
have many of the attributes of antique furniture, gold, or diamonds,
in that they are unlikely to drop greatly in value. They also have
the attributes of manufacturing industry, because they produce
marketable products. The fact that the return on the capital
investment is relatively small is not now such a disadvantage, if the
capital asset is almost certain to maintain or increase its real value.

There is, particularly at a personal level, a natural desire to have
one's cake and eat it now rather than at some distant point in an
uncertain future. On the other hand, there is a certain reassurance
in investing in something which is likely to retain its value during
the foreseeable future; if society wishes to have a secure future it
must make such investments. The more secure the investment, the
less need there is to discount future values when estimating their
present worth. This implies that, in 'real' terms (i.e., over and
above any effects of the changing value of currency), a lower
discount rate should be used when assessing the value of investments with little risk than when assessing the value of more risky
enterprises. Rather than the figures of ten per cent, five per cent,
or even three per cent currently used in some quarters, figures of
one per cent or even less may often be appropriate. A figure of
one per cent is in fact used by the Swedish Forest Service, and
that is in a country where forestry plays a major role in the
national economy and which is widely regarded as a model of
efficiency and logical planning.

It must be emphasized that the long-term nature of forestry
does not mean that it is, for that reason, a poor investment.
Particular plantations, certain actions, or particular methods of
management may be uneconomic, but well-managed woodlands
of a reasonable size, on suitable sites, should give worthwhile
returns. A higher discount rate should be used in making investment decisions where tree species which are susceptible to attack
by pests or disease are grown or where there is a high risk of
windthrow or fire. Under the most risky conditions likely to be
considered for forestry investment purposes, discount rates of
five per cent or even higher may be appropriate. Alternatively,
it may be advisable to reduce the predicted future income, to
allow for the uncertainties involved, if a low discount rate is used.

An appropriate discount rate will need to be based on the
judgement of the owner's forestry adviser, and its selection may
be a little subjective. However, a seriously considered judgement
on this issue is likely to provide better guidance than the use of an

arbitrary and possibly irrelevant 'standard' rate.

Having discounted future costs and returns at an appropriate rate, it will then be possible to compare these on an equal basis in order to assess the attractiveness of investment in planting, fertilizing, cleaning, or other activities; or to compare the attractiveness of woodland investment with investments in other enterprises. The higher the ratio of discounted income to discounted costs, the more attractive will that particular investment be.

4. COSTS

a) Land

In most cases the value of land is related to uses which do not consume or destroy it. The purchase price of land can, therefore, perhaps best be regarded as a capitalized rental for the use of that land in perpetuity, the land itself being 'owned' by the nation or State.

The price paid for land on the open market is a reflection of demand; which is influenced by the general economic climate, by the structure of taxes and grants, by short-term fluctuations in the price of farm crops, and by many other factors. Bare land for afforestation currently sells at prices comparable to low-grade agricultural land, even the most productive forest land being unlikely to fetch more than about twenty per cent of the price of the best agricultural land. At first sight this may seem strange, but while agricultural land will yield crops within a year of purchase, bare forest land will take at least 50 years before it starts to yield a normal return. It is, therefore, more sensible to compare the value of fully stocked agricultural land with that of forest land bearing an even spread of young and old timber. In this case the values ought to be closely comparable over the middle range of land types, with agricultural land being more highly valued than forest in the better farming areas, and the reverse being the case in some of the poorer farming areas (Table 4).

Table 4 — Typical values of land and crops
(£ per hectare, 1982)

	Uplands and poor soils	Middle quality agricultural land	Best quality agricultural land
Forestry:			
land	400	750	1000
growing stock, roads, fences, buildings	2000	3000	3000
total	2400	3750	4000
Agriculture:			
land	400	3000	5000
livestock, crops, fences, buildings	200	1000	1000
total	600	4000	6000

In fact, market prices for fully stocked forest land often fall short of the figures given in Table 4, but under ideal circumstances these figures should be realistic. Assuming that the land and the growing stock maintain their value on the open market, there should be no need to debit the woodland account with any figure for rental or interest on capital. However, as there is always likely to be some element of risk through disease, pests, or falling market prices, it may be reasonable to include a small figure as an annual rental figure on the growing stock. On the prices given in Table 4 an annual rental of about £20 per hectare would seem a reasonable general figure for well-stocked woodlands, this being slightly over one per cent of the capital value in upland areas and rather less than one per cent elsewhere, where the risks are usually less. Somewhat different figures will of course be applicable in some circumstances. If such a rental figure is included in calculations it can replace the use of discounting procedures.

b) Supervision and labour

Depending on the size and distribution of individual woodlands, the type of crop, and the method of management, one qualified forester (with a diploma or degree in forestry) will be able to supervise anything between 500 and 1500 hectares of woodlands. Taking an average figure of 1000 hectares, and assuming that the forester is paid roughly twice the basic minimum manual wage, he will cost the equivalent of approximately 3 to 4 basic working man-hours per hectare per year. This figure will include the preparation of a Working Plan for each woodland or group of woodlands, the maintenance of records, preparation of financial estimates, progress reports, and liaison with the Forest Authority. It will in most cases also include the marking, measurement, and sale of timber, and overall supervision of labour.

Each gang of men may also have a foreman or working forester in charge, who may carry out some of the marking and measurement of timber as well as the day-to-day supervision of routine planting, weeding, and so forth.

If timber is sold standing and the maintenance of forest roads is carried out by contractors, the amount of labour required will not be very high. The amount of planting, fencing, weeding, cleaning, pruning, fire control, and pest control will vary considerably from place to place (these operations will be examined in greater detail in Chapter 11). As a general guide, however, these operations will require between 5 and 10 basic working man-hours per hectare per year. One thousand hectares of woodlands will therefore require between 3 and 7 men for these tasks. If road maintenance is also carried out and timber is felled and extracted to roadside, where it can be loaded onto lorries, the number of men required will be increased by a further 7 to 15, depending on the volume of timber and the difficulty of extraction.

At 1982 prices, the costs of managing 1000 hectares of woodlands are likely to be roughly as follows:

supervision: 1 man (+ overheads and vehicle)	£15 000
labour (planting, etc.): 5 men (including 1 foreman)	£40 000
materials (plants, etc.)	£10 000
labour (felling, etc.): 12 men (including 1 or 2 foremen)	£110 000
use of machinery	£56 000
	£231 000

or about £230 per hectare, employing 1 man for every 55 hectares.

(Income should be somewhere between £200 and £500 per hectare, the actual figure depending very much on the standard of management over the past 50 years or more. But there are many cases where income is less than expenditure, and is likely to continue so for various reasons.)

5. SILVICULTURAL SYSTEMS

Before considering the costs or values of particular operations or particular aspects of woodland management it will be useful to consider different systems of silviculture. There has in fact been only one system in common use in the British Isles in recent years, namely the clear-felling system. There have been good reasons for this; not least the fact that we emerged after a century of cheap imports and two World Wars with very little standing timber and little tradition of woodland management. The emphasis since then has been on the planting of bare land and on clearing and re-planting derelict woodland and scrub. Other silvicultural systems can be used, however, and may often be more appropriate than clear-felling. The main features of these different systems have recently been reviewed (Helliwell, 1982), and the following paragraphs are taken from that review.

Many different systems of growing and harvesting trees have been used over the years ... some being more suitable for certain species, climates, soils, or economic conditions than others. Modifications or variations continue to be developed ... as new restraints or demands are made upon the forest, and further developments will no doubt occur in the years to come.

In the first instance, silvicultural systems can be divided into even-aged and uneven-aged systems (Figure 1), each of which can be further sub-divided, and so on. Some systems will, in practice, be intermediate between those listed; for example, a clear-felling system which leaves some mature trees to shed seed will resemble a shelterwood system to some extent, and the boundary between the two systems will be somewhat vague. Similarly, a clear-felling system which uses very small felling areas will tend to resemble a group selection system.

The *clear-felling system* (Figure 2) involves the growing of trees for a certain length of time and then clearing them all at once, leaving the area to be re-stocked by planting, natural seeding, or coppice growth from the old stumps. Some thinning will usually take place at intervals during the life of the crop, to enable the final crop to grow without undue interference, and, usually, to provide some saleable produce.

The *shelterwood system* (Figure 3) is similar to the clear-felling system, except that the final crop trees are removed in two or more stages over a period of about 5 to 30 years instead of all at one time. The young crop (usually from natural seeding)

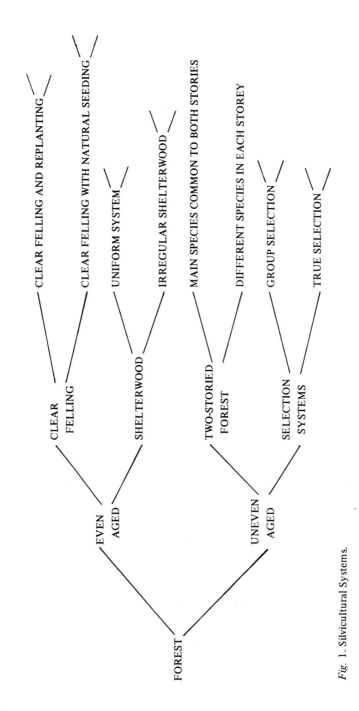

Fig. 1. Silvicultural Systems.

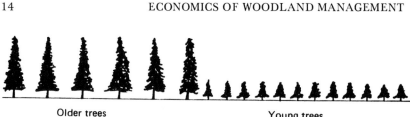

Older trees   Young trees

Fig. 2. Clear Felling System.

Old crop heavily thinned   Young crop becoming   Young crop established.
prior to regeneration   established. More of   All mature trees
                               the mature trees removed   removed

Fig. 3. Shelterwood System.

Fig. 4. Group Selection System.

Fig. 5. Selection System.

is, therefore, established under a partial tree canopy. The establishment of the young crop may be more reliable or less costly (under some circumstances) than after clear felling, but the removal of the last of the older trees may be more difficult; and the system cannot be used unless the mature trees are deeply and firmly rooted — which rules it out over much of upland Britain, and some lowland areas as well.

The *group selection system* (Figure 4) resembles a very small-scale clear-felling system, whereby each stand or compartment of the forest has, ideally, a full range of age-classes, distributed in small groups. The size of the groups may vary from as little as two or three mature trees (i.e., perhaps 100 to 200 m^2) to as much as a quarter or half hectare (2500 to 5000 m^2) or more.

The *selection system* (Figure 5) in its ultimate form, is based on the individual mature tree as the unit of silvicultural treatment. Each area of forest is visited about every five to ten years, according to the rate of growth of the trees, and selected trees are removed, including some large trees and some smaller ones. Re-stocking is a continuing process and is usually obtained from natural seeding, but may be by planting in some instances.

The effects of these different systems may be summarized very briefly as follows:

1. There are some indications that some soils may be adversely affected by pure crops of some tree species, particularly if the trees are grown at close spacing and with little or no thinning;

2. Even-aged pure crops do not encourage a very wide diversity of plants and animals; they may increase the risk of serious outbreaks of pests and diseases; and they are not very attractive to look at;

3. There is little to choose between different silvicultural systems in terms of total timber volume produced, but even-aged systems tend to produce a greater proportion of small-sized material, which is of lower unit value (Figure 6);

4. Shelterwood systems are likely to be ruled out over much of the British Isles due to the risk of windthrow;

5. The cost of harvesting timber may be as much as fifty to ninety per cent of total costs, and may be increased by the use of mixtures of species or uneven-aged silvicultural systems. Such increases can, however, be justified if the benefits, in terms of increased timber value, decreased risk of pests, increased amenity value, etc., exceed the increase in costs.

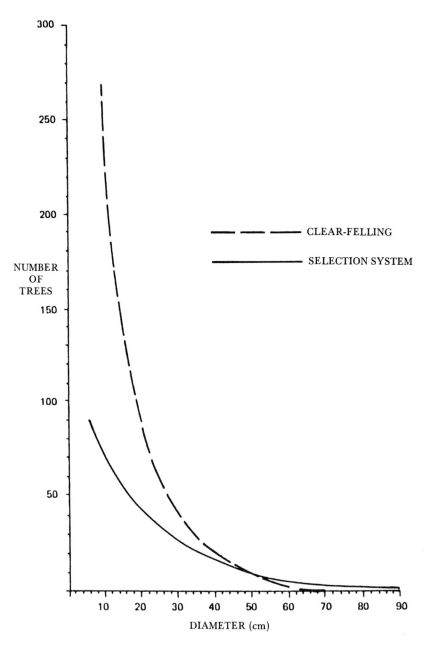

Fig. 6 — A comparison of the numbers of trees of different sizes
removed under clear-felling and selection systems

This summary is, of course, very simplified. It will, however, indicate the main features of different silvicultural systems, insofar as these affect the economics of woodland management.

6. TIMBER PRODUCTION

a) Size of enterprise

Most woodland produce is relatively low in value per tonne when it leaves the woodland. One tonne of timber loaded onto a lorry at roadside is likely to be worth enough to pay one man's wages (plus overheads) for between 3 and 10 hours working time, or between 1 and 3 hours working time for one man plus an expensive item of heavy machinery. A team of two or three men, with equipment which is likely to cost more than their pooled annual income, have therefore to be able to fell, extract, and load at least 10–20 tonnes per day if there is going to be sufficient income left to pay for the planting and tending of the trees and yield an overall profit to the owner.

Each lorry load of timber, of between 10 and 20 tonnes, will be destined for a particular mill or factory and will need to contain only material of a certain specification. This specification will normally cover the tree species and the size and quality of the timber.

The economics and practicalities of factory production require a steady flow of logs into the factory yard. Suppliers with a large and regular flow of timber of the appropriate specification are therefore able to negotiate contracts to supply timber more readily than suppliers with only a small or irregular flow. It is, of course, usually possible to channel supplies through a woodland cooperative or a round timber merchant, but these will expect some return for their time and trouble, and the merchant may not always be interested in parcels of timber that are of below average quality, of low total volume, or which are in woods with poor access.

There are, therefore, advantages in having a large forestry enterprise, where there is a large and regular output of timber of each major specification. In such cases the workforce, whether directly employed or contracted, can be equipped with suitable machinery, which can be kept fully utilized, and the felling, extraction, loading, and delivery of timber can then proceed in a regular and efficient manner.

Assuming that the woodlands are producing around twelve cubic metres of timber per hectare per year, in a range of sizes and qualities, from firewood to prime planking or veneer timber, a minimum size for a self-contained timber-producing enterprise is probably about 300 hectares. That would be sufficient to employ two or three men and their machinery permanently, with firewood being sold separately to local merchants, and the occasional parcel of very large timber being sold standing to specialist mills or merchants. A larger area, of 500 hectares or more, would enable all timber to be handled by a larger and more fully equipped team of men (although firewood would still be dealt with separately in most cases). An even larger area, of around 1000 hectares or more, would also provide greater flexibility in working, for there are always some areas which are difficult to work during wet weather, and demand for any one particular size or species of timber may fluctuate from year to year, making it advantageous to have some flexibility in the output of different assortments of timber.

Where a woodland enterprise is too small to market its own timber it will usually be able to do so through a woodland co-operative or through a round timber merchant. These will involve some small cost, but the effect on the overall economics of the woodlands is likely to be relatively small, when compared, for example, with the effects of the size and accessibility of each woodland.

b) Size and distribution of individual stands

A woodland enterprise should be contained within as small a geographical area as possible for efficient timber production. A single large block would be ideal, but some degree of fragmentation can be accepted without incurring very great additional costs, provided that the costs of fences and roads are shared equitably with the intervening properties. If fragmentation becomes too great, however, costs will rise accordingly. Travelling time for men and machines will be increased, and the organization of full loads of each type of timber will be more difficult if each woodland or stand of timber is small and widely separated from the next stand of similar type.

Approximate comparative costs of felling and handling timber are given in Table 5. These are only intended as a very broad guide, and will vary in detail according to the methods used and the local conditions.

Table 5 — Comparative costs of felling, extracting, and loading timber on a woodland estate of 10 000 ha in areas of different size and distribution

Size of individual woodlands (ha)	Geographical spread (km^2)			
	100 (Parish)	500 (District)	2500 (County)	12 500 (Region)
1000	1	1.1	1.2	1.3
100	1.1	1.3	1.6	2
10	1.3	1.7	2	3
1	1.8	2	3	4

The costs of other operations such as planting and weeding will also increase in a roughly similar manner, although not quite so steeply. The cost of fencing will increase more steeply, with decreasing woodland size. As the felling and handling of timber represents a large proportion of the cost of producing timber, the figures in Table 5 may be taken as a fair representation of the overall comparative costs of producing timber in woodlands of different sizes.

The economics of subdivision within the woodland, into stands of smaller sizes, is likely to follow roughly the same pattern. But there may also be gains, in better utilization of the site, production of more valuable assortments of timber, easier establishment of young crops, aesthetic benefits, better wildlife conservation, and other factors, which may outweigh the increased costs.

This may present a disappointing picture to those who would like, for various reasons, to see more small woodlands in the landscape. Timber production is, however, an industry like farming or motor-car production, where similar economies of scale are to be found. This is not to say that small woodlands cannot be justified in some instances, but the economics of timber production do not favour them.

c) Harvesting methods
One reason why the harvesting of timber is less expensive in large compact woodlands is that more efficient harvesting methods can be used. Larger and more expensive machinery can be effectively employed, with a high percentage of working time and relatively little time wasted in travelling from one job to the next. Machinery of any size or description will in fact be employed more efficiently in a larger woodland than in several smaller woodlands several miles apart. In the days when timber was felled with hand tools

and hauled to local markets by teams of horses (which was not very long ago in terms of tree growth), the advantages of large woodlands were not so great. Under present circumstances, however, the more efficient harvesting methods in use in large forests in Scandinavia and North America are capable of producing more than two tonnes of stacked timber per man-hour, compared with figures of around half a tonne per man-hour for timber of comparable type in smaller scattered woodlands, using smaller machines and proportionally more labour. Even after allowing for the additional cost of the larger machines, the cost of harvesting a tonne of timber in the larger forests is still likely to be less than half that in smaller woodlands.

Other factors also influence harvesting methods and costs; particularly the nature of the terrain. Flat well-drained land presents few problems, and timber can be brought out by relatively cheap tractors. Land which is steeply sloped, irregular, or boulder-strewn presents greater problems, and requires one or more of the following:

i. a fairly dense network of fairly expensive roadways;
ii. use of winches and cables to move the timber from stump to roadway, which is time-consuming and expensive;
iii. use of expensive articulated four-wheel-drive tractors, capable of working on irregular terrain.

Where the ground is poorly drained and soft it may be necessary to use crawler tractors with wide tracks, which have a low ground pressure.

The type of silvicultural system adopted may also affect the harvesting methods employed, and their cost. However, the differences are likely to be relatively small under British conditions, where the terrain is rarely suitable for the use of very large machines. Provided that an adequate road network is provided, and extraction lanes are made at frequent intervals in the crop, the overall savings in cost associated with clear-felling systems are likely to be small or non-existent. There are several reasons for this:

i. clear-felling systems (as compared to selection systems) typically produce a larger amount of very small thinnings in the early stages of each rotation, which are difficult and expensive to fell and extract, and are also of little value as timber, compared to larger sizes of log;
ii. clear felling often requires subsequent clearance of branches before re-planting can take place; in other systems, branches can often be left where they lie or merely moved to one side;

iii. clear felling often results in the whole site being subjected
to pressure from heavy vehicles, which can produce com-
paction of the soil and subsequently poor growth of trees.
It is better, on such sites, to restrict vehicles to clearly
defined routes, as happens during thinning or selective felling.

There are *some* advantages in clear felling, the main one being
that work is concentrated on a small area of land, and a relatively
large amount of timber is removed at the time of clear felling. In
the case of very small isolated woodlands it may be impossible to
market timber profitably under any other system, and thinnings
may have to be left to rot, or be sold very cheaply to a local firewood merchant if they are of suitable (i.e., broadleaved) species.

d) Timber prices

The price that the woodland owner receives for timber is the
residual value that is left when all the costs of felling, extraction,
hauling, handling, sawing, and processing are deducted from the
selling price of the finished product. In the case of a high-value
product such as furniture timber there is much more likelihood
that this residual value will be greater than zero than with low-
value products such as chipboard, paper pulp, mining timber, or
fencing material.

Taking some typical examples, the production of various timber
products is broken down into its component costs in Table 6.

Table 6 — Typical costs (£) of producing timber products (1982)

	Firewood	Fencing posts	Sawn softwood	Sawn hardwood
Standing value of trees (per m^3)	4	10	20	60
Cost of felling	4	4	3	4
Cost of extraction	5	5	4	5
Cost of haulage	5	5	5	5
Cost of sawing, etc.	8	26	48	76
Price of finished product	26	50	80	150

Taking one species of tree, oak, as an example, the standing
value of a typical parcel of timber may range from virtually nothing
to £200 per cubic metre, according to the size and quality of each
tree (Table 7). Most other species have a smaller range of value
than this, with the upper price ranges being absent, and with less
material falling into the lowest grades. Prices for a typical coniferous (softwood) species are given in Table 8.

Table 7 — Typical prices of standing oak timber of different size and quality
(£/m³ in 1982)

Veneer butts over 1 m diameter and 2.5 m length	£200
Veneer butts over 85 cm diameter and 2.5 m length	£150
Plank butts over 75 cm diameter and 2 m length	£120
Plank butts over 55 cm diameter and 2 m length	£100
2nd grade over 55 cm diameter	£60
3rd grade over 55 cm diameter	£25
Mining timber	£13
Firewood	£4

Table 8 — Typical prices of standing spruce timber of different sizes
(£/m³ in 1982)

Average tree volume (m³)	Price per m³ (£)
0.05	2
0.10	3
0.15	4
0.20	5
0.30	8
0.40	10
0.50	11
0.75	13
1.00	15
2.00	18
3.00	20
4.00	20

With price differentials of this magnitude it is obviously in the owner's interests to grow timber of reasonably large size and high quality, if this can be achieved without undue cost.

The price paid for timber will obviously depend to some extent on the distance of the woodland from the sawmill or factory. Prices of timber from woodlands in regions with few timber-using industries will tend to be low, to allow for the increased cost of transporting it to the mill. For example, timber grown in Cornwall or the Hebrides is likely to fetch several pounds per cubic metre less than similar timber in Gwent or Dumfries, and small-sized or low-quality material may be very difficult to sell in such areas.

7. NATURE CONSERVATION

Woodlands form one of our richest habitats for wild plants and animals, and nature conservation is often a main or subsidiary object of management, particularly in woods which have existed without significant interruption for many centuries, and which are usually the most valuable in this respect.

a) Size and distribution of woodlands

Many woodland birds and mammals require a minimum area of woodland, and are unlikely to be found in very small woods or copses. Similarly, very small woodlands may not present suitable conditions for the long-term survival of populations of some woodland plants, insects or molluscs. However, most of the British woodland flora and fauna is capable of existing in woodlands of around 5 to 10 hectares, for we have lost those species such as wild boar, lynx, wolf, and bear which require large areas of forest. Even very small woodlands of 1 hectare or less can provide a suitable habitat for many species, if suitably managed, particularly if they are fairly close to other woodlands. Therefore, although a large wood is likely to be more valuable than a small wood, the value per unit area is likely to be fairly similar for woods of all sizes above 5 or 10 hectares, with the value per hectare depending more on the type of management than on the size or shape of the woodland.

b) Tree species

Different tree species provide habitats for different assemblages of insects, lichens, mosses, and, in some cases, birds and mammals. For example, some insects occur only on particular species of trees, and some birds and mammals rely heavily on the seeds of particular tree species. The overall diversity of plants and animals in a woodland is, however, also strongly influenced by the physical structure of the woodland, and by the fertility of the soil.

A mixed oak/ash/lime/maple woodland of fairly open and varied structure is likely to be of high value for nature conservation, and a dense even-aged plantation of exotic evergreen trees is likely to be of relatively low value, but if the evergreen plantation were of more open structure and contained a small proportion of native deciduous trees its value would probably be much enhanced.

Bearing this in mind, it may nevertheless be useful to divide tree species into three main groups (with reference to the British Isles), as in Table 9.

Table 9 — Value of different tree species for nature conservation

---

I. *High value*
Native species with diverse insect populations, regular seed production, or other useful attributes: e.g., oak, willows, poplars, thorns, lime, birch, alder, Scots pine.

II. *Medium value*
Native species not included above, and some introduced species: e.g., ash, holly, beech, hornbeam, sycamore, larch.

III. *Low value*
Most other introduced species.

---

c) Silvicultural systems and methods

As indicated above, the presence of particular tree species is often less important than the overall structure and management of a woodland. Several factors are important:

i. the presence of well-developed vertical layers, which gives the greatest number of different niches for wildlife including, ideally,
   a. tall trees;
   b. smaller trees;
   c. bushes and saplings;
   d. tall herbs;
   e. short herbs and mosses.

ii. diversity of tree species and types; a mixture of two or three main species, including some deciduous and some evergreen trees, will be advantageous — there is, however, no very great advantage in having more than two or three main tree species, in the British Isles — and management becomes very difficult where there are many more than this number;

iii. the presence of old, rotten, or dead trees; these provide habitats for hole-nesting birds and a large range of insects, fungi, lichens, and mosses.

Selection, or group selection, systems give greater structural diversity within each stand than does clear felling. It is often argued that clear felling gives such diversity over a whole forest; but the scale of this diversity is then so large that it benefits only the largest birds and mammals and the more mobile plant species, and does little for the smaller or less mobile species. It is also easier to obtain a continuity of old or dead trees in a selection forest than in a clear-felling situation, and mixtures of tree species are often easier to manage under a selection system.

Shelterwood systems are intermediate in many of these respects.

d) Valuation of benefits

Some things, such as nature conservation or the visual beauty of the countryside, are not usually valued explicitly. That is not because they have no value, or are 'above' such mundane matters; or because they are incapable of being valued. The reason lies in the fact that they can not readily be bought and sold as discrete items. There is therefore no market for them, as there is for personal goods or services such as shoes, books, or hot meals, for example.

There are, however, other methods of valuation which are no less valid than the use of market prices (which can themselves give a misleading indication of the true value of a commodity in some instances).

Nature conservation is something that affects a large number of people, both now and in the future. It may be of value for several reasons, including education, research, plant breeding, pest control, and sheer enjoyment. It is therefore of benefit to the community as a whole, rather than just to the owner of a particular piece of woodland, and it should be valued on that basis.

The placing of a value on the contribution which nature conservation makes to the long-term benefit of society will be a question of placing priorities on items such as national security, food supply, medical services, housing, or freedom of speech, and must therefore involve political and social, as well as economic decisions. There will obviously be upper and lower limits. Few people would claim that nature conservation should be accorded a zero value, and few would claim that it should have greater priority than the prevention of starvation, for example. Between these limits, however, some agreed order of priorities must be obtained.

Once an approximate order of priorities has been agreed, on a national or international basis, some framework is then necessary for subdividing the total national 'value' between the different areas of land and water in the country. It is also preferable for a monetary figure to be attached to such values, so that they can be included in calculations and decision making on an equal footing with timber prices, planting costs, and other factors.

Let us assume that the overall value of nature conservation in Britain has been given a figure of £20 000 million, in order to arrive at decisions which most people would regard as sensible (Helliwell, in press). This gives an 'average' value per hectare of around £1000, for this purpose. The value of any one particular hectare will then depend on its difference from the 'average', in terms of numbers of plants and animals present, their numbers, their scarcity in the region and the world, and any particular research, educational, or aesthetic value associated with them; all of which are capable of being compared on a reasonably object-ive basis.

Many woodland areas may be valued at over £5000 per hectare on such a basis, whereas others may be valued at £500 or less. In the former case it will be in the nation's long-term interests to ensure that such values are not jeopardized by short-term gains in timber production; and this may involve payment of compen-sation, the use of special tax allowances, or other financial assist-ance to the owner. The development of easily measured parameters for valuation purposes is the main difficulty in such a process, apart from the inevitable reluctance of any nation to spend money or forgo income to provide long-term benefits. In cases where a woodland has been designated a Site of Special Scientific Interest (SSSI) by the Nature Conservancy Council, there are provisions under the *Wildlife and Countryside Act* 1981 for the payment of grant aid to owners following an agreed plan of management.

As indicated earlier, some silvicultural systems and practices may be more favourable to the conservation of particular types of wild plants and animals than are other systems. However, leaving some trees to die and rot, planting a mixture which includes native tree species, or leaving occasional open glades may incur some loss in revenue from timber production. Such losses should, ideally, be balanced against gains in nature conservation values, at least in a very approximate way, and the woodland owner should in some way be compensated for such losses.

8. AMENITY AND RECREATION

Woodlands have long been managed as hunting preserves, land-scape features, or as areas in which to walk, play, or camp. In a few cases their value for such purposes clearly outweighs any returns from timber production, although timber is also likely to be produced as a secondary product.

a) Size and distribution of woodlands

In a landscape with very few woodlands, each additional woodland is likely to be of benefit to the amenities of the area, if it is suitably sited and appropriately managed. On the other hand, in a landscape which is totally forested each additional *clearing* will add to the amenity of the forest. Peak values appear to be reached, in most cases, when fifty to sixty per cent of the landscape is wooded.

If, in a landscape with a small percentage of woodland, there is a choice between one large woodland and several smaller woods, then the greatest amenity is likely to be afforded by the smaller woodlands. This, of course, runs directly contrary to the efficient production of timber, but where amenity has a high priority it may have greater weight. Such a situation is likely to be found in our better farming regions, where land values under agriculture are higher than forest land, but where there is still some call for woodlands, for nature conservation, amenity, and recreation. Under such circumstances isolated copses and belts of trees can provide a considerable amenity without greatly reducing the area under agriculture. Economic calculations must, however, take amenity value into account, for such woodlands are unlikely to be very profitable as a purely timber-producing enterprise, even with generous government grants for tree planting.

The overall pattern of woodlands in the landscape should of course be sympathetic to the scale and form of the land, fields, and other features.

b) Tree species

Within very broad limits it matters little what particular species of tree are grown. However, the general *type* of tree is important in many cases, particularly when grown as a pure crop, and it is probably sufficient to distinguish five such types:

    i. broadleaved trees casting a dense shade, e.g., beech, sycamore, lime;

    ii. broadleaved trees casting a light shade, e.g., oak, birch, ash;

    iii. deciduous conifers, e.g., larch;

    iv. evergreen conifers casting a dense shade, e.g., spruce, hemlock fir, silver fir;

    v. evergreen conifers casting a light shade, e.g., pines.

The use of evergreen conifers in areas dominated by broadleaved woodland may need to be handled with caution, and the mixture of different types or species of tree in any sort of regular pattern is best avoided if the woodland can be seen from above. On the other hand, large areas of a single species can be monotonous, and some variation, following natural changes in slope, elevation, or soil type, will help to relieve such monotony, particularly if the boundaries between species are not too sharply defined. Mixtures of types (e.g., larch and pines, or birch and spruce) can also be attractive if the mixture is of a random rather than a regular appearance.

c) Silvicultural systems

The system of silviculture employed is, again, at least as important as the tree species used, and is often more important. Large-scale clear felling creates ugly, if temporary, bare patches in the land-scape, and destroys the sense of permanence, which is a highly valued attribute of the landscape. Small paths and tracks tend to become lost or 'rationalized', and the forest changes from that of Goldilocks and the Three Bears to that of the twentieth century pulp factory. Some landscapes lend themselves more easily to clear felling than others, and, in large-scale relatively featureless land-scapes with continuous forest cover, clear-felled areas may provide welcome open spaces and give variety to an otherwise monotonous view. Such situations are, however, the exception rather than the rule in the British Isles. In most cases the structural and visual variety provided by a selection or group selection system will give the most attractive appearance.

Careful public opinion surveys have been carried out which indicate that the general form of the forest can be more important than the actual tree species present. A spruce forest can be beautiful if appropriately managed, and an oakwood can be monotonous and uninteresting at certain stages of its development if grown in a very uniform manner.

d) Valuation of benefits

The valuation of amenity is subject to similar difficulties to those encountered in valuing nature conservation. The time-scale is a little shorter and the variety of uses is, perhaps, not so wide, but the parameters for assessment of value are less easy to define. The main factors influencing the visual attractiveness of a landscape are given in Fig. 7. The contributory factors are, themselves, not easy to measure objectively, although in most cases they can be assessed fairly consistently by subjective appraisal. However, any assessment of value must include some measurement of the numbers of

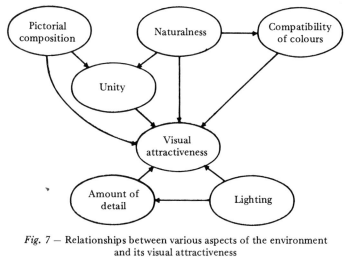

Fig. 7 — Relationships between various aspects of the environment
and its visual attractiveness
(taken, with some modification, from a paper by Helliwell (1978) in
Landscape Research **3**, 3)

people involved and the value which they derive from the landscape. This value will depend partly on a person's familiarity with
a particular landscape, the proximity of similar landscapes, and the
numbers of other people present, in addition to its aesthetic
quality. Such factors are not always easy to define or measure in
a meaningful way.

As with nature conservation, it would be useful to have an
'average' amenity value for an area of woodland, which could be
used as a yard-stick for the assessment of particular areas. Some
system, such as that suggested by the present author in 1967 (see
Appendix 1), would be useful.

9. FORESTRY AND OTHER LAND USES

Woodlands and forests can affect the functioning of other land
uses in a number of ways.

a) Water supplies

At one time forestry was a favoured land use in water catchment
areas, as it avoided undue siltation or biological pollution of the
water. However, it is now realized that forestry can have some
disadvantages, as the total amount of water flowing into the river
system is often less than under comparable areas of grassland or
moorland. There can also be increased siltation if ploughing,

draining, roadmaking, and timber extraction are not carefully controlled.

The most serious of these effects is likely to be the reduction in stream-flow. Trees intercept a certain amount of precipitation, which then evaporates without reaching the ground. Trees also abstract moisture from the ground and lose it to the atmosphere at a greater rate than some other types of vegetation. The net result is that many afforested catchments yield less water than non-forested catchments. The pattern of flow may also be altered to some extent, often resulting in a more even flow, with less water after sudden storms and more water in periods of drought, but this depends very much on the particular soil types involved. The type of tree and management may also be important, with evergreen trees having a greater effect than deciduous trees.

The amount of silt carried by streams can affect the useful life of reservoirs, if these become significantly reduced in volume due to siltation, and the added care needed to avoid excessive siltation may increase the costs of forest management in such areas.

Where water catchment is a major consideration, the afforestation of large areas may require the construction of additional storage reservoirs or boreholes, or the adoption of water-saving devices by industry. This fact must then be included in any calculation of costs and benefits related to forest management.

Forests in some parts of Britain may reduce water yields by between half a million and one million gallons per hectare per year. At 1981 prices, this may represent a cost of anything between about £20 and £80 per hectare per year, if the forest is in a catchment area.

b) Farming

Farming and forestry have, in recent centuries, been completely separate enterprises in most parts of the British Isles. In some other countries this is not the case, where it is simply one of several enterprises in which the farmer is involved. There are often considerable benefits to be gained from integration of forestry with animal or crop husbandry, but most recent trends are towards increasing specialism in fewer enterprises.

The benefits to be derived from the integration of farming and forestry can take several forms:

    i. better use of land of varying quality, by using each area of land for the enterprise to which it is best suited;

   ii. the use of surplus summer grazing land for forestry, without any significant reduction in the numbers of stock on the farm;

  iii. an increase in the number of enterprises on the holding, and a consequent reduction in the likelihood of financial difficulty if the price of any one product falls;

  iv. the sale or lease of part of the holding for forestry purposes, to raise capital for the improvement of the remaining farm enterprise;

   v. improved shelter for lambing areas, winter grazing, and crops;

  vi. increased flexibility in deployment of labour;

 vii. an overall increase in labour requirements and economic and social activity in the neighbourhood;

viii. increased financial flexibility, as, unlike most farm products, timber sales can be brought forward or delayed by a few years, to provide income when it is most needed.

It is also possible, in some instances, for animals to graze (or crops to be grown) between newly-planted trees or within widely-spaced plantations, thereby maximizing the total out-turn from the land.

The main difficulty stems from the need to have a sufficient area of woodland to warrant the employment, on a full or part-time basis, of skilled management, labour, and machinery. Alternatively, if the management is placed in the hands of a woodland co-operative or contracting company, integration becomes more difficult in some respects. In either case, the owner must have an active interest in both farming and forestry if a joint enterprise is to succeed.

It is difficult to quantify the benefits of integration, but in some circumstances they could increase the profit margin considerably, give greater financial stability, greater amenity value, and increased gross income. These benefits are likely to be greatest in upland or marginal farming areas.

c) Hunting and shooting

The existence of many of the woodlands and forests in Britain and other countries is due to their value for hunting or shooting. At one time, large areas were kept as hunting reserves for royalty and other wealthy people. At the present time, fox hunting, pheasant shooting, and the less organized shooting of pigeons, squirrels, rabbits, and hares, often provide a reason for planting or retaining wooded areas. The amount of meat obtained from shooting is small, but the owners, or their shooting tenants, often place considerable value on this activity, and in many parts of Britain estates with woodlands suitable for hunting or shooting have an appreciably enhanced market value.

In recent years deer (of several species) have become more numerous in Britain and often need to be controlled if excessive damage to trees and agricultural crops is to be avoided. Venison fetches a good price on local or foreign markets, and income from selective culling can help to supplement the income from woodlands.

d) Fishing

The planting of trees close to the banks of streams and ponds can affect fish stocks. An ideal situation is a patchy growth of broad-leaved trees near to streams. A total lack of tree growth gives insufficient shade to the water in summer, and a complete woodland cover tends to give too much shade and too much leaf fall. The planting of coniferous trees close to water is not, in general, beneficial, as the water which is shed from the foliage tends to be acidic and to contain various slightly toxic substances. Also, the leaf-litter of most conifers is relatively unpalatable to the larger aquatic organisms and tends to accumulate in the water. Bacterial decomposition can then lead to a lack of oxygen and the death of fish.

10. TREE SPECIES AND TIMBER PRODUCTION

a) Volume and value

Some sites will not give rapid growth of any species, due to the lack of adequate rainfall, poor soil, or extreme climatic conditions, and under such conditions it may be difficult to justify any forestry operations if the sole object of management is timber production.

Other sites will give rapid growth of softwoods up to a certain size, when there develops an increasing risk of the trees being blown down, due to poorly-drained soil and exposure to strong winds. Under these conditions most of the timber produced is likely to be small and of fairly low value per cubic metre.

More favoured sites will give rapid growth up to larger sizes. On such sites it may not always be desirable to select the fastest-growing species, as, particularly when grown quickly, these are often of low density and fail to meet the requirements of structural or joinery timber, and are therefore suitable only for lower-grade purposes such as packing cases or pallets.

Where the site is suitable, the most profitable general market is likely to be that for structural timber. In recent years there has been relatively little home-grown softwood timber suitable for this purpose, but with the increasing volume of conifer sawlogs now coming out of British forests (and which is due to double over the next 15 to 20 years), there will be increasing penetration of this market by home-grown timber. Table 10 gives some comparative volumes and values for timber of different species grown under typical plantation conditions.

Table 10 — Comparative annual volume production and value of different tree species on different sites
(m³/ha/yr; £/m³; and total value, free-on-lorry at 1981 prices)

Species	Poor site*			Medium site			Productive site		
	m³	£/m³	Total	m³	£/m³	Total	m³	£/m³	Total
Scots pine	6	10	60	9	14	126	12	22	264
Corsican pine	8	10	80	12	15	180	18	20	360
Lodgepole pine	6	10	60	9	14	126	12	20	240
Sitka spruce	8	10	80	15	15	225	22	20	440
Norway spruce	8	10	80	14	18	252	20	24	480
European larch	4	12	48	8	14	112	12	24	288
Japanese larch	4	12	48	8	14	112	12	24	288
Douglas fir	10	12	120	16	16	256	22	22	484
Western hemlock	12	12	144	16	16	256	22	20	440
Red cedar	12	12	144	16	16	256	22	22	484
Grand fir	15	10	150	20	14	280	28	16	448
Noble fir	12	10	120	16	14	224	20	18	360
Oak	4	10	40	6	25	150	8	40	320
Beech	4	8	32	7	20	140	10	30	300
Ash	4	8	32	8	20	160	12	40	480
Southern beech	10	10	100	14	20	280	18	30(?)	540(?)
Poplar	6	10	60	9	20	180	12	30	360

* The term 'poor site' refers to each species. For example, a 'poor site' for western hemlock may be a 'medium site' for lodgepole pine. Conversely, a 'poor site' for Sitka spruce may be totally unsuitable for grand fir, oak, ash, or poplar.

b) Markets and prices

Markets and prices are subject to change from time to time, but the general pattern changes only slowly. The market for small-sized, bent, or excessively knotty timber is likely to remain much poorer than that for straight logs 30 cm or more in diameter. Much of the demand for wood chips (for the manufacture of particle board, pulp, and other purposes) can be met from the off-cuts and other waste from the milling of timber, and the price for such uses is likely to be related to the cost of this 'waste' timber. Wherever possible, therefore, the aim should be to produce the maximum volume of saw logs and the minimum volume of pulpwood and other low-priced timber. Typical markets for various sizes and types of timber are given in Table 11.

Table 11 — Typical markets and standing prices for various sizes and types of timber ($£/m^3$, 1981)

Species	Diameter 5 – 20 cm		Diameter 20 – 30 cm		Diameter 30 cm +	
Spruces and pines	pulpwood) chipboard) fencing)	0 – 5	boxes) pallets) planking)	10 – 20	planking) boxes) pallets)	25 – 35
Larch	fencing	5 – 15	sawn fencing	15	boatskins	25 – 50
Douglas fir	fencing	0 – 5	boxes) pallets)	10 – 20	planking	25 – 35
Oak	firewood fencing pulpwood	0 – 3 3 – 5 0 – 4	fencing	6 – 8	fencing planking veneer	10 – 25 25 – 125 130 – 200
Beech	firewood turnery pulpwood	0 – 3 5 – 10 0 – 4	various	10 – 20	planking	20 – 40
Ash	firewood turnery	0 – 4 5 – 10	handles hurdles	5 – 10 5 – 10	planking veneer	30 – 60 60 – 80

c) Windthrow

The problem of windthrow (that is, the blowing down of trees) before the trees reach optimal size is widespread in northern and western parts of the British Isles, particularly where soils are poorly drained and where high windspeeds are common. On such sites the choice of tree species is limited to those which can grow under these particular conditions of soil and climate. In most cases this means Sitka spruce or lodgepole pine, neither of which is particularly wind-firm. A mixture of birch and alder may help to stop windthrow from spreading within a spruce or pine plantation, but the main lines of defence are likely to be:

    i. wide initial spacing;
    ii. the avoidance of thinning;

iii. early felling, and

iv. the creation of a more wind-firm structure in the forest, rather than any major change in timber-producing species.

The economic consequences of early windthrow have already been mentioned. These consequences are made all the worse by the difficulty of harvesting a tangled mass of fallen trees, and the difficulty of finding labour and markets to handle a sudden additional out-turn of timber after an extensive blow.

d) Pests and diseases

As compared to agricultural crops, there has been relatively little selection and breeding of timber trees. This means that most woodlands and plantations contain a fairly broad spread of genetic variability, which makes them less vulnerable to attack by pests and disease than highly selected crops. The situation may change somewhat if present trends towards greater selectivity continue.

A more immediate cause for concern stems from the use of trees outside their natural range. This gives an unstable situation, as the pests and diseases which affect the tree in its natural range have usually reached some sort of equilibrium with each other and the host species. If planted outside this range, the tree may be subject to unusual climatic conditions, which may favour particular pests or diseases; and the normal checks and balances that operate on particular pest species may be absent outside the natural range of the host tree. This is especially likely to be the case where trees are grown in extensive monoculture rather than in a mixture with other species.

One of the functions of woodland management is to forestall or curtail damage by pests and disease. This is not the place to describe them in detail. However, major pests include the grey squirrel, various species of deer, rabbits, hares, voles, aphids, and several species of moth and other insects. These, and various diseases, such as butt-rotting fungi or blister rust, may influence the choice of species, and the method and costs of management. Very often the choice of a particular tree species or silvicultural system will increase the expected income from timber sales, but at an increased risk of damage by pests or disease. Any financial calculations should therefore include an increased risk factor, or an amount of money to cover the cost of preventive measures.

11. FORESTRY PRACTICE

a) Ploughing and draining

A certain amount of ploughing and draining is often needed, particularly when establishing plantations on upland or heathland sites which have not carried a tree cover in the last 100 years or more. Ploughing loosens the soil, buries some of the vegetation, and gives better conditions for the establishment of young trees. The cost is usually fully repaid by easier and cheaper costs of planting and weeding, in addition to the more rapid growth of the trees. Costs per hectare are likely to be around £100 to £150, with outputs varying between 0.1 and 0.4 ha per hour, depending on conditions and the type of tractor and plough.

Deep ploughing at 2 m or 4 m spacing also provides furrows which help to drain the site, although on heavy clays and some peats these can act as barriers to the lateral growth of tree roots and cause instability when the trees reach 10 or 15 m height.

Additional or deeper drains may also be needed, to prevent water flowing into the site from higher ground, to act as main drainage channels, or to lower the general water table (although the latter objective is not always attained). Costs are likely to be around £0.30 to £0.40 per metre, or anything from £20 to £100 per hectare, depending on the length of drains, their depth, and ease of cutting. A back-acting digger should dig between 30 and 40 m of drains per hour.

b) Plants and planting

The small (10–30 cm) sizes of coniferous trees commonly used in forestry cost around £60 to £100 per thousand, or around £150 to £250 per hectare. Broadleaved trees tend to be more expensive, costing, on average, about twice as much as conifers. Delivery, handling, and planting are likely to cost about as much as the plants.

Under some conditions, such as on ploughed peat, where little weed growth is expected, very small 1-year-old seedlings can be used which are cheaper to purchase and easier to plant, reducing costs by around fifty per cent.

On very fertile sites with considerable weed-growth but few problems of exposure to wind, larger plants are often used, costing up to ten times as much as the smaller plants. Wider spacing and reduced weeding costs may help to offset the increased planting costs, particularly in small isolated woodlands which are relatively costly to weed. An approximate indication of planting costs is given in Table 12.

An additional allowance of ten or fifteen per cent is often made, to cover the cost of replacing trees which die in the first year.

Table 12 — Approximate costs of planting, expressed in man-hour equivalents* per hectare

	Spacing	Costs		
		Plants	Planting	Total
1 yr. seedlings (conifers)	2 × 2 m	20	20	40
2 or 3 yr. transplants (conifers)	2 × 2 m	35	40	75
2 or 3 yr. transplants (broadleaved)	2 × 2 m	70	50	120
Whips, approx. 1 m high (mainly broadleaved)	3 × 3 m	70	50	120

* at 1982 prices, one man-hour cost about £5, including overheads.

The savings to be obtained by using self-sown rather than planted trees are not very large in most cases. However, self-sown seedlings often grow more quickly and with less damage from deer and other animals, and they often require less weeding. The expense of cleaning and thinning may be greater, but where such 'natural regeneration' occurs readily, it can afford some saving in cost. This is particularly true in small woodlands and in uneven-aged forests, where planting areas are not concentrated in large units.

c) Weeding and cleaning

Weeding involves the cutting or killing of unwanted herbage, bracken, or shrubs during the period when the planted trees are very small. On some sites or under some conditions no weeding is needed. On other sites it can be very expensive, even with modern herbicides. Table 13 gives approximate costs for weeding under a variety of conditions. These costs will be spread over the first 2 to 5 years after planting.

Table 13 — Approximate costs of weeding (man-hour equivalents per hectare)

Soil fertility	Percentage tree cover			
	0	20	40	60
Very fertile or calcareous	100	60	30	10
Medium fertility	50	25	10	—
Low fertility or very acidic	10	5	—	—

Other variables will also influence the cost, including whether or not the ground has been ploughed, the number of trees per hectare, the size of the plants, any local restrictions on the use of herbicides, and the type of weeds present, but the main variation is likely to follow the pattern shown in Table 13.

Cleaning involves the removal of unwanted woody growth, after weeding has ceased and before the first commercially viable thinning. The amount of cleaning needed depends on the thoroughness with which weeding has been carried out, the number of self-sown or coppice-stool shoots of unwanted woody species, and the rate of growth of the crop trees in relation to the unwanted species. In many situations no cleaning will be required, but in other cases two or three cleanings may be needed, often costing more than the weeding.

d) Brashing and pruning

Brashing involves the removal of branches on the lower 1.8 metres of the stem of the tree, usually before the first thinning. This enables inspection and marking of thinnings to be carried out, and makes thinning easier. It is also the first stage in pruning trees to produce knot-free timber. It is an expensive operation, and the cost is sometimes reduced by brashing only the larger trees, or every second or third row. Where line-thinning is practised, brashing may be omitted completely, access being gained by removing complete lines of trees rather than selected trees from every row.

Pruning involves the removal of branches to a height of around 5 to 8 metres, to produce a butt length of knot-free timber. This is usually done in several stages, when the stem attains between 8 and 10 centimetres diameter, and is most needed when growing broadleaved trees at wide spacing. At one time, broadleaved trees were commonly planted at around 1 metre spacing in order to produce stems with few side branches. This was expensive and took a very long time to produce a stem of large girth. Modern practice is to plant at about 2 metres spacing, or wider, and to prune some or all of these trees. The potential difference in value between pruned and unpruned hardwood timber makes pruning well worth the cost in most cases. In the case of most coniferous trees the situation is less clear, as the present market for knot-free logs does not always give a much greater price than the market for similar trees with knots. One exception is larch, which is relatively easy to prune and is, at the present time, still used for the outer skins of small fishing vessels and similar craft. Typical costs of brashing and pruning are given in Table 14.

Table 14 — **Typical costs of brashing and pruning**

Tree species	Brashing 2000 trees per ha to a height of 1.8 m (man-hours/ha)	Selective pruning of 200 trees per ha, up to 6 m (man-hours/ha)
Spruce	40 – 60	18 – 22
Pines	25 – 50	16 – 20
Douglas fir	30 – 60	16 – 22
Larch	20 – 40	14 – 18
Broadleaved trees	(not usually needed)	8 – 10

e) Thinning

Unless trees are planted at very wide spacing and pruned, as is common practice with poplars, some thinning will be needed before the trees reach their largest size. An exception might be on sites where windthrow is known to be a problem. On such sites a common practice is to plant at a fairly wide spacing (e.g., 2.5 x 3 m), or to reduce trees planted at 2 x 2 m to about 1000 per hectare before the branches of adjacent trees have become interlocked. The plantation is then left unthinned until it is judged to be in imminent danger of blowing down, when it is clear-felled.

Ideally, thinning should be done frequently, every 2 to 5 years, removing a relatively small number of trees each time. In that way there is least risk of windthrow, the timber produced is of an even texture, and maximum productivity is achieved. However, the economics of timber harvesting favour heavier thinnings at less frequent intervals, with only 3 or 4 thinnings during the life of the crop rather than 8 or 10 or more. The optimal number will depend on ease of access, the extraction methods used, and the price obtained for the timber.

There is often an unfortunate tendency to delay thinnings, because of depressed markets, shortage of labour, or lack of managerial initiative. In most cases this is likely to be detrimental to the long-term profitability of the woods, and should be avoided as far as possible. A delay of a year or two is acceptable, but delays of 10 or 20 years are not unknown, resulting in loss of income from thinnings, a reduced amount of growth of the better trees, and problems with windthrow when delayed thinning takes place.

Comparative costs of harvesting thinnings of different sizes are given in Fig. 8. When the poor prices obtained for small-sized

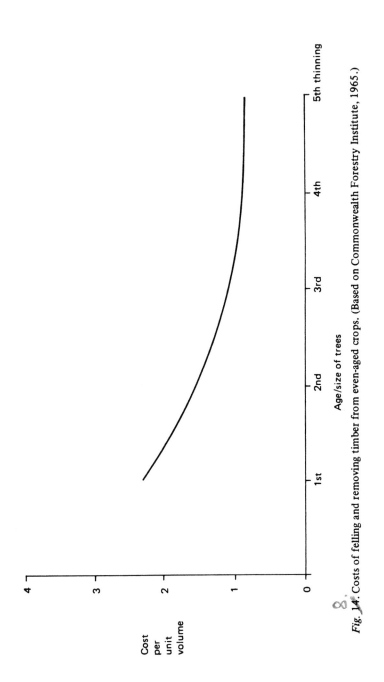

Fig. 14. Costs of felling and removing timber from even-aged crops. (Based on Commonwealth Forestry Institute, 1965.)

timber are also considered, it is evident that the marketing of small-sized thinnings in small, inaccessible, or otherwise difficult woodlands is not an easy task, and may sometimes have to be carried out at a loss.

The costs of marking and measuring thinnings are dealt with in section (j).

f) Felling and extraction of timber

With the development of modern lightweight power saws, the felling and trimming of trees represents a fairly minor item in the total cost of producing timber. There are large machines which cut trees by means of hydraulic pincers or a circular saw and then pick them up and cut the branches off. These need large areas of uniform terrain in order to work efficiently, and they are unlikely to play a very major part in British forestry, except in the larger forests.

Costs of felling and extraction have already been mentioned in Chapter 6.

g) Fencing and pest control

Fencing may be needed to prevent farm animals entering woodlands and damaging young trees, to curtail the movements of deer, hares, or rabbits, or, occasionally, to indicate property boundaries or to restrict public access.

Under English law, it is normally the duty of the owner of farm animals to prevent them from straying and causing damage. It is also a question of common sense that, other things being equal, the costs of stock-proof fencing should be borne by the farming enterprise and not by the forestry enterprise. After all, trees do not need a fence around them to prevent them from straying!

In practice, however, it is often agreed that the costs of fencing should be borne by the forestry enterprise. Where the two enterprises are integrated under one management it makes little difference which enterprise pays, except that it may make one of them appear to be more profitable than it really is, and *vice versa*. It is also simpler in many cases for the forestry enterprise to construct and maintain the fence, particularly if it is designed to keep out wild animals as well as domesticated animals, as it is the forester and not the farmer who has the greatest interest in keeping animals out of vulnerable woodland areas.

The costs of fencing small or irregular-shaped woodlands are very high in proportion to their area (Table 15), which is another factor which favours larger woodlands. Where there are no farm animals it may be possible to manage woodlands without fencing, although individual young trees may then require protection against hares or rabbits. In the case of woodlands of less than 1 ha the costs of fencing may well be more than fifty per cent of total management costs.

Table 15 — Approximate costs (in man-hour equivalents per hectare per year) of maintaining fences around square woodland areas of different sizes

Area (ha)	Cattle	Sheep	Type of fence Rabbit/hare	Roe deer	Red deer
0.1	28	35	35	57	82
1	9	11	11	18	26
10	2.8	3.5	3.5	5.7	8.2
100	0.9	1.1	1.1	1.8	2.6
1000	0.3	0.4	0.4	0.6	0.8

The question of whether or not to fence against deer, hares, and rabbits depends very much on:
   i. the numbers of animals present;
   ii. the amount of food available to them, other than the planted trees;
   iii. the size and shape of the areas to be regenerated;
   iv. the type of tree being planted (or self-seeded).
On large wooded estates, overall control of the numbers of animals, coupled with appropriate choice of species and silvicultural methods, should reduce or eliminate the need for fencing.

On small estates surrounded by other woodland areas, there may be less opportunity to control the numbers of animals.

Fencing is not, of course, effective against grey squirrels, which damage trees (particularly beech and sycamore) by stripping bark from trunks or branches of about 10 to 20 centimetres diameter. Squirrels can either be accepted, or they can be controlled by trapping or poisoning. Total elimination is rarely possible for any length of time, as the animals can travel several miles in search of new territory, and control measures must be carried out each year if they are to be effective. Half-hearted control is likely to be a waste of time and money.

Trees planted in extensive areas of thick grassy vegetation may also be damaged by a sudden increase in numbers of mice or voles, which chew the bark around the base of young trees and thereby kill them. In such cases the best course of action is likely to be the elimination of the grass by use of a suitable herbicide.

Other pests of trees against which measures are frequently taken are beetles which infest the stumps of felled conifers and then emerge to feed on young trees. On extensive clear-felled areas it is usually necessary to treat planted conifers with an insecticide, to prevent damage.

Other pests (such as pine looper moth, larch sawfly, green spruce aphid, oak-leaf roller moth) and diseases (caused mainly by various fungi) can affect trees from time to time. In most cases the trees will suffer some reduction in growth, but actual control measures are not usually necessary. *Precautionary* measures are often taken, and include the painting of conifer stumps with a solution of urea immediately after felling (to reduce the incidence of butt rot), and the prohibition of the lighting of fires in conifer stands (to reduce the incidence of 'group dying'). Such measures may add a little to the total cost of forest management, but are likely to be relatively insignificant.

Costs of controlling deer and other animals, where they are not excluded by fencing, can vary considerably. In some cases, high prices may be paid for stalking or for venison, but the employment of trained staff to supervise the stalking and to cull surplus animals is likely to cost more than the income from these sources. Some approximate costs of pest control are given in Table 16.

Table 16 — Typical net* costs of pest control in
forest areas of 500 ha or more
(man-hours/ha/year)

	Low cost	High cost
Deer: Red or Sika	0.3	0.7
Fallow	0.4	0.8
Roe	0.5	1.0
Muntjac	0.3	1.0
Hares	0	0.5
Rabbits	0	0.5
Grey squirrels	0	0.8
Voles	0	0.1
Bark beetles	0	0.1

* after allowing for any income from shooting permits and
meat, and excluding costs of fencing.

h) Forest roads

Roads are needed within the forest to enable timber to be removed. They may vary from a simple bulldozed track to expensive roads involving blasting, earthmoving, and laying of crushed stone. The amount of roadway needed and its cost will depend on several factors, including the steepness of the ground, the softness of the ground surface, and the availability and proximity of stone. Generally speaking, the more roads there are the easier will be the subsequent management. Woods with insufficient or inadequate roads are often impossible to manage profitably.

A hill sheep farm can be run, after a fashion, with no internal roads, but in that case the produce *walks* off the hill. In the absence of roads there may be no economic way of getting timber out of a woodland area.

Where roads are expensive to construct it will usually be best to have a minimal road network, of around 1 or 2 kilometres per 100 hectares of forest, and to use relatively expensive methods of timber harvesting such as 'skyline' winches. Where roads can be constructed more cheaply, densities of up to 5 or even 10 kilometres per 100 hectares may be economically justifiable. Some typical costs for forest roads are given in Table 17.

Table 17 — Typical costs of forest roads
(£ per kilometre, 1981 prices)

| Type of terrain | Construction | | Annual maintenance cost |
	Low cost*	High cost**	
Gentle slope			
Deep peat	5000	15 000	100
Well-drained soil over soft or fissile rock	2000	4000	100
Well-drained soil over hard rock	3000	6000	100
Poorly-drained clay over soft or fissile rock	4000	7000	150
Poorly-drained clay over hard rock	5000	9000	150
Steep slopes			
Soft or fissile rock suitable for road surface	4000	7000	200
Soft or fissile rock unsuitable for road surface	5500	10 000	250
Hard rock, requiring blasting and crushing	6000	9000	150

* Low cost = road suitable for small tractors, Landrover, etc.
** High cost = road suitable for lorries and timber trailers.

With road densities varying between 1 and 10 kilometres per 100 hectares, and annual maintenance costs at about 25 to 60 man-hour equivalents per kilometre per year, each hectare of forest is likely to carry an annual road maintenance cost of around 2 to 3 man-hour equivalents. This is in addition to the initial cost of road construction, which is a capital item similar in many respects to the cost of the land or the purchase of a growing forest.

i) Fire precautions

Forest fires are most likely to occur in extensive areas of young planting, before the trees have grown sufficiently to suppress grasses and other ground vegetation. The trees themselves rarely burn if there is not a layer of dry vegetation at ground level to sustain the fire, and large areas of new planting on former grazing land are particularly vulnerable.

Most forest fires in the British Isles are started by people, by spreading from heather-burning, stubble-burning, campfires, cigarette ends, or by deliberate mischief or malice. Lightning can also start fires, but is usually accompanied by rain, which prevents the fire from spreading. Broken glass or old bottles are reputed to have started fires occasionally, but there is usually little evidence to support such claims.

The best precaution against fire is to avoid having a dense or extensive growth of grass or other vulnerable vegetation. 'Firebreaks' may be made, to reduce the spread of any fire which may occur, by containing it within a limited area. Such 'breaks' may be strips of bare ground or areas of less vulnerable forest. At one time bands of Japanese larch were often planted in upland areas as fire-breaks, as they grow relatively quickly after planting and suppress ground vegetation within about 10 or 12 years. The trees themselves, like most deciduous trees, are also less inflammable than evergreen conifers.

It is difficult to give a general figure for the cost of fire precautions. In many situations it will be extremely low, or nil. The cost of insurance against fire is likely to be equivalent to about one man-hour per hectare per year. In vulnerable areas this figure should be approximately doubled, to include the costs of maintaining fire-breaks, fire-beaters, watch-towers, and patrols during periods of high risk. In highly vulnerable areas used by the public, this figure may need to be increased even further.

j) Yield control and timber measurement

There are various ways of selling timber and various methods of measuring and controlling the output of timber from the forest. Perhaps the simplest system was the old coppice system, whereby a proportion of the total area was cut each year, on a rotational basis, and the purchaser paid an agreed sum per acre for the produce. Modern production of pulpwood, on a coppice system or using conifers on a short rotation, presents a similar picture, but with the produce being paid for on a weight basis, after going over a weighbridge at the mill.

In both these cases production is controlled by cutting so many hectares each year, and there is no need to carry out any very extensive measurement of standing or felled timber.

Where timber is sold by volume, some sort of measurement must take place, before or after felling; and in cases where several grades of timber are involved, the measurement and grading must be done with considerable care. In the case of thinnings this measurement may be carried out during the process of selection and marking of the trees, or as a subsequent operation.

In mixed or uneven-aged crops the situation is more complicated, and it may be necessary to carry out a complete enumeration of each area of forest every few years, measuring all the trees above a fairly small minimum size. In this way a complete picture of the growth rate and current growing stock is obtained, enabling marketing to proceed on a regular and continuing basis without suddenly finding that there is a shortage or a surplus of trees of a particular size or species. A complete enumeration of this sort could take about 3 man-hours per hectare per year, and in most cases some sort of sampling procedure will be used in order to reduce the time taken.

In the case of even-aged crops the amount of measurement needed for adequate control of timber yield will be considerably less, and on small woodland estates little formal control is likely to be needed.

Table 18 lists approximate costs for marking, measuring, and selling timber under a range of conditions.

Table 18 — Approximate costs of marking, measuring, and selling timber (man-hours*/ha/year)

	Marking	Measuring	Selling	Total cost
Woodland estate of 50 ha:				
Unthinned coppice or pulpwood	0	0	0.2	0.2
Even-aged conifers	0.4	0.1	0.3	0.8
Even-aged hardwoods	0.3	0.1	0.3	0.7
Uneven-aged mixed woodland	0.5	0.2	0.4	1.1
Woodland estate of 1000 ha:				
Unthinned coppice or pulpwood	0	0	0.1	0.1
Even-aged conifers	0.3	0.1	0.1	0.5
Even-aged hardwoods	0.2	0.1	0.1	0.4
Uneven-aged mixed woodland	0.4	0.3	0.2	0.9

* the man-hours should be charged at 50% to 100% more than the basic rate, as skilled manpower is needed. At 1982 prices, each man-hour should therefore be charged at £7 to £10.

12. OWNERSHIP AND MANAGEMENT

a) Types of woodland ownership

The type of ownership under which a woodland exists will influence the objects of management and, to some extent, the economic attractiveness of various options. It may be of interest to list some of the many types of woodland owner:

> small farmers;
> large agricultural estates;
> individuals with money to invest;
> investment syndicates;
> wood-using industries (uncommon in Britain);
> charitable trusts (e.g., the National Trust,
>   the Woodland Trust);
> family trusts;
> Parish and District Councils;
> insurance funds;
> National Park Authorities;
> State forest enterprise (the Forestry Commission
>   in Britain);
> churches.

The main object of woodland management may range from nothing, in the case of many farmers who have inherited or acquired farms which include small areas of woodland, to the positive creation of an asset of growing value which has certain tax advantages. The financial resources, tax liabilities, and requirements of each owner are likely to differ significantly from those of neighbouring owners, so that what is economically advantageous to one owner may be less so to another.

On the other hand, the very long-term nature of forestry makes it difficult or impossible to implement sudden major changes in management practice without disrupting the viability of the enterprise. There are basic rules of 'good practice' which it would be foolish to ignore. Weeding, cleaning, and thinning should not be neglected, and timber should not be allowed to become very much over-mature and thereby rotten and worthless. In other words, the basis of a productive forest enterprise should be maintained, as it takes several decades to re-create it once it is lost.

b) Foresters, agents, consultants, and contractors

Another variable factor in management lies in the personnel employed to manage woodlands. In some instances the owner may manage the woods himself (or herself), with assistance from regular or contract labour. In other cases he may leave most of the management to a forester, land-agent, or consultant, or to a woodland co-operative or a forestry management company. The quality of management varies considerably and is not always directly related to the cost.

In many respects an ideal situation would be for the routine management to be carried out by a resident forester or land agent, under the overall control of a consultant. The consultant would, together with the owner, formulate the management strategy and give advice on silvicultural methods and marketing. At the present time this rarely happens.

On small woodland estates it may sometimes be difficult to justify the expense of even very occasional visits by a consultant. On woodland estates of between 100 and 500 hectares, where only a small permanent staff is employed, some regular input from a well-qualified person is clearly needed, and can usually be justified in financial terms. On larger estates the forester (or management company) responsible for day-to-day management is likely to be seen as fully competent. Even there, however, there may be some advantage in employing an independent consultant, to provide a second opinion, wider knowledge, or fresh ideas. The cost of this is not likely to exceed 0.1 to 0.25 man-hour equivalents per hectare per annum on a large estate, and even a very small increase in long-term productivity should more than cover that cost.

In short, the owner should not be satisfied with mediocre management if his woodlands exceed 50 or 100 hectares, and even below that size he should obtain skilled advice if at all possible.

Whether the actual work of planting, weeding, felling, and so on should be done by permanent employees or by contractors depends on local conditions. In many cases a trustworthy regular local contractor is the most satisfactory solution. Unskilled or unscrupulous contractors can be troublesome and can do considerable damage to standing trees during felling and extraction of timber, but contractors are usually cheaper than direct labour for most operations. On the other hand, it is useful to have at least one or two direct employees who can carry out odd bits of planting, weeding, and cleaning which are too small to be worth employing a contractor, and who can undertake general maintenance of ditches, fences, hedges, gates, and roadways, and keep a look out for fires, stray sheep and cattle.

c) Woodland accounts

Where woodlands are managed on a commercial basis, accounts of income and expenditure must be kept for tax purposes. In addition to these accounts, some fairly detailed annual assessment of the value of the growing stock may also be useful, as it will provide a much more complete picture of the state of the enterprise, particularly in years when the value of timber sold is less than or greater than normal. This annual valuation will be carried out as an adjunct to the manager's yield control procedure, and should not add greatly to the cost. With large enterprises, information on each woodland compartment may be stored in computer-readable form and periodically amended, enabling production forecasts and financial statements to be produced very easily.

The placing of a value on an area of woodland is not a simple matter, as there are a number of conceptual difficulties involved, but, provided that some reasonably sensible procedure is consistently employed, a realistic and useful financial statement should be obtained.

A typical woodland area of around 100 hectares might have the following costs and values:

Value of woodlands at commencement of year	£200 000
Value of woodlands at end of year	£228 000
Income from timber sales £17 000	
Costs £20 000	
'Rental' £ 2000	

Apparent return on investment = ~~13.5%,~~ 11.5% [handwritten] made up by:

effects of inflation	+ 10%
increased real value of growing stock	+ 4%
'rental'	+ -1%
current year's accounts	- 1.5%

Thus, although the current year's accounts show a deficit, the enterprise as a whole shows a net gain.

one/ [margin note] In the absence of inflation, this enterprise would show a net return of ~~five~~ two [handwritten] and a half per cent on the capital investment in addition to the basic one per cent 'rental' appropriate to that particular type of forestry.

Temporary fluctuations in the price of timber should not be taken into account in assessing the value of the woodlands, but they will obviously influence the current year's accounts.

d) Cash flow

The greatest single difficulty in running a woodland enterprise such as the one described above is the absence of cash flow during the formative years. If the enterprise is one of several enterprises this may not be a serious problem, but if it is the main or sole enterprise under that ownership then the deficit in current income is likely to be a problem.

This is one reason why most farmers do not consider planting new woodlands or rehabilitating areas of scrub, even if the long-term economics are favourable. Arrangements whereby the land is afforested under some form of partnership with someone wishing to make a long-term investment seem to be the most promising means of avoiding this problem. The investor will pay the full cost of afforestation, and may also pay an annual sum to the farmer, as rent, or as the farmer's share of the net profits, based on an annual valuation of the growing stock. The farmer will provide the land and, possibly, some of the labour for fencing, planting, and maintenance.

e) Grants and taxes

Grants are currently available in Britain for various types of tree planting. At the time of writing they do not cover more than a moderate percentage of the planting costs, and contribute less than ten per cent to the total cost of growing standing timber (and no more than three per cent of the costs of growing and producing timber 'free-on-lorry'). The main influence of these grants may therefore be more psychological than financial.

The tax system has a much more dominant effect on forestry. One basic problem of forestry stems from the fact that a commercially viable forest enterprise has a high capital value, and society generally does not like to see too much wealth in the hands of a few individuals. Forestry in Britain is treated reasonably favourably as regards Capital Transfer Tax, as commercial woodlands can qualify for Business Relief (50%), and payment of the tax on the timber (but not the land) may be deferred until the timber is sold; but on even a relatively small woodland estate of 100 hectares, and where the owner has no other assets of any sort, this tax could take twenty to twenty-five per cent of the standing value of the produce from these woods. Where the estate is larger or the owner has other major assets the incidence of this tax could rise to as much as forty per cent of the gross income. For this reason it seems likely that woodland ownership will increasingly move from the hands of private individuals and families to institutions such as insurance companies and processing industries, which are not liable to be faced with this tax.

On the other hand, forestry is treated very favourably as regards Income Tax. Under Schedule B, which is the normal Schedule for woodlands, the amount of tax paid is negligible. Moreover, the owner can elect to have particular woods taxed under Schedule D, whereby he can offset the cost of establishing a young plantation against income from other sources, and thereby reduce his overall tax liability. Such areas will then be taxed at the full rate when they come into production, but can revert to Schedule B if the ownership changes. The practical effect of the Schedule D option is to favour:

i. clear felling and replanting, rather than any other silvicultural system;
ii. investment by people with large taxable incomes;
iii. investment by 'absentee investors' (who can easily sell the property and thereby allow it to revert to Schedule B when convenient), rather than by resident landowners;

iv. use of short, rather than long, rotations (also favoured by the present Capital Transfer Tax and the new planting grants).

Some of these effects are not always desirable, and some change in the tax system would, in the author's opinion, be beneficial. Such changes might involve a reduction or elimination of Capital Transfer Tax on the value of growing timber (but not the land); removal of the Schedule D option, except (in agreed cases) on land that has not carried commercial woodland recently; and an increase in liability for income tax on annual profits (though not so high as to discourage sensible thinning and felling when it is due).

13. THE FUTURE DEMAND FOR WOODLAND PRODUCTS

All the forecasts of the FAO and other bodies are for world short-ages of timber within 20 years or less. Timber is one of our few renewable raw materials; unlike coal, oil, natural gas, and metalli-ferous ores, which are present in finite quantities. It is very versatile, and can be used to make plastics, paper, sugar, alcohol, and other chemicals, in addition to its use for structural and decorative purposes. As other materials become more difficult and expensive to extract or manufacture, timber is likely to be in greater demand and to fetch higher prices.

The type of timber which seems likely to be in greatest demand is straight, evenly-grown, fairly knot-free softwood timber of around 30 to 40 centimetres diameter. There is also likely to be a continuing demand for good quality hardwood timber, and a large, but less lucrative, market for timber of any size or shape for fuel, chipboard, paper pulp, and the chemical industry.

The need for woodlands to be managed in such a way as to provide habitats for a diversity of wild plants and animals is likely to become greater rather than less; and the need for wood-lands for screening purposes or improvement of the landscape is also likely to increase.

It would therefore seem reasonable to think in terms of around fifty per cent of the upland areas of Britain coming under forest within the next 100 years, and around ten per cent of the low-land areas, giving a figure of about thirty per cent for the country as a whole. This is about three times the present woodland area, and would involve some (relatively small) loss of potential agri-cultural production. However, we are in no great danger of being short of food; and we could be completely self-sufficient even on this reduce acreage, if it ever becomes necessary, merely by changing to a slightly more vegetarian diet. We are, on the other hand, in grave danger of being short of industrial raw materials within the next 100 to 200 years.

An expanded forest area of this magnitude, increasing at something around one per cent per annum for several decades, would require very sensitive handling if it were to be socially and environmentally acceptable, but this should not be impossible, given suitable political direction and adequate resources. The Forestry Commission has been criticized in the past for its lack of sensitivity, but much of the blame for this must be laid at the feet of HM Treasury and the Government, who have held the purse strings and issued directives governing policy and financial restraints. However, it is a little strange that the Forestry Commission still remains completely committed to the clear-felling system as its only basic silvicultural system, when the Forest Services of several other European countries favour other systems to a much greater extent. A more flexible approach to woodland management is needed, with figures being assigned to the value of amenity, recreation, and nature conservation, as well as to timber production and job provision. Forestry could, and should, play a more prominent role in Britain in the future than in recent centuries and could help to make us less dependent on imported timber and wood products, which at present account for more than five per cent of our total import bill.

USEFUL BOOKS AND PAPERS

Crowe, S. (1978) *The landscape of forests and woods.* Forestry Commission Booklet 44. HMSO, London.

Forestry Commission (1978) *Forestry practice* (9th edition). Forestry Commission Bulletin 14. HMSO, London.

Forestry Commission (1978) *Standard time tables and output guides.* Forestry Commission Booklet 45. HMSO, London.

Harding, D. M. (1978) The hidden input: water and forestry, in *The future of Upland Britain*, ed. R. B. Tranter, 91–99. Centre for Agricultural Strategy, University of Reading.

Hart, C. E. (1979) *Taxation of woodlands.*

Hart, C. E. (1979) *British timber prices and forestry costings.* (Both the above are published by Dr. Hart, at Chenies, Coleford, Gloucester GL16 8DT.)

Helliwell, D. R. (1974) Discount rates in land-use planning. *Forestry* 47, 147–152.

Helliwell, D. R. (1976) The effects of size and isolation on the conservation value of wooded sites in Britain. *Journal of Biogeography* 3, 407–416.

Helliwell, D. R. (1982) *Options in forestry*; a review of literature on the effects of different tree species and silvicultural systems on soil, flora, fauna, visual amenity, and timber production. Packard Publishing Ltd., Chichester.

Helliwell, D. R. (in press) *Assessment of priorities in nature conservation.* Packard Publishing Ltd., Chichester.

Jansson, A.-M. and Zucchetto, J., *et al.* (1978) *Energy, economic and ecological relationships for Gotland, Sweden.* A regional systems study. Ecological Bulletins No. 28, Swedish National Science Research Council.

Mutch, W. E. S. and Hutchison, A. R. (1980) *The interaction of forestry and farming.* Dept. of Forestry and Natural Resources, University of Edinburgh.

Pimentel, D. and Pimentel, M. (1979) *Food, energy and society.* Edward Arnold Ltd., London.

Scottish Woodland Owners Association (1978) *Forestry management accounting.* Timber Growers Scotland, Edinburgh.

Sinden, J. A. and Worrell, A. C. (1979) *Unpriced Values: Decisions without market prices.* John Wiley and Sons, Inc., New York.

Tree Council (1976) *An evaluation method for amenity trees.* Tree Council, London.

Troup, R. S. (1928) *Silvicultural systems*. Oxford University Press.
Walker, D. A. (1979) *Energy, Plants and Man*. Packard Publishing Ltd., Chichester.

USEFUL ADDRESSES

Arboricultural Association, Ampfield House, Ampfield, Romsey, Hampshire — maintains a list of approved consultants and contractors able to deal with amenity trees and tree surgery; also holds meetings and publishes a journal.

British Trust for Conservation Volunteers, 10–14, Duke Street, Reading, Berkshire — organizes working parties of volunteers to undertake tasks of value to nature conservation.

Forestry Commission, 231, Corstorphine Road, Edinburgh EH12 7AT — the official government agency which administers State forests, carries out applied research, and controls grant payments.

Institute of Chartered Foresters, 22, Walker Street, Edinburgh EH3 7HR — the main professional forestry body in Britain, publishing a technical journal and holding meetings for professional foresters; issues a list of members in consultancy practice.

Institute of Terrestrial Ecology, 68, Hills Road, Cambridge CB2 1LA — includes the former research branch of the Nature Conservancy and the Institute of Tree Biology, with several research stations in England, Wales, and Scotland; carries out research on a range of topics, many of which are relevant to forestry.

Irish Forestry Society, c/o Royal Dublin Society, Ballsbridge, Dublin 4 — publishes a journal and holds meetings.

Nature Conservancy Council, 19, Belgrave Square, London SW1X 8PY — gives advice on management for nature conservation and in certain cases gives grant aid for appropriate management.

Royal Forestry Society of England, Wales, and Northern Ireland, 102, High Street, Tring, Herts. HP23 4AH — publishes a journal and holds meetings.

Royal Scottish Forestry Society, 1, Rothesay Terrace, Edinburgh EH3 7UP — publishes a journal and holds meetings.

Royal Society for Nature Conservation, 22, The Green, Nettleham, Lincoln LN2 2NR — parent body of the local and county Nature Conservation Trusts, many of which have full-time conservation officers who are able to advise on management for nature conservation.

Timber Growers Scotland Limited, 6, Chester Street, Edinburgh
EH3 7RD — represents woodland owners in Scotland, and
manages woodlands for some of its members.

Timber Growers England & Wales Limited, Agriculture House,
Knightsbridge, London SW1X 7NJ — represents woodland
owners in England and Wales.

Tree Council, 35, Belgrave Square, London SW1X 8QN – co-ordin-
ating body for matters relating to trees in the landscape.

The Woodland Trust, Westgate, Grantham, Lincolnshire NG31 6LL
— a charitable organization which acquires woodland for amenity
and conservation.

GLOSSARY

Amenity: Visual attractiveness, as seen from roads or paths or
distant viewpoints.

Broadleaved tree: Tree with broad leaves, e.g., oak, birch, holly.

Compartment: A unit of woodland of fairly uniform character-
istics for management purposes. Usually between 2 and 20
hectares.

Conifer: Tree bearing cones, and not bearing true flowers or fruit.

Coppice: Areas of woodland which are cut periodically and
allowed to grow again from shoots which sprout from the cut
stump. (Few conifers have this ability, but most broadleaved
trees will do so.)

Coupe: Area of woodland felled at any one time.

Deciduous trees: Trees which shed their leaves in winter.

Evergreen trees: Trees which retain their leaves throughout the
year.

Free-on-lorry: (Timber) which has been felled, extracted from
the woodland, and loaded onto a lorry.

Hardwoods: Broadleaved trees, or their timber.

Hectare (ha): 2.471 acres, or $10\,000\,m^2$, or $0.01\,km^2$.

Man-hour equivalent: Cost or value equal to the cost of employing one man for 1 hour's working time; including allowances
for holidays, sickness, travelling time, insurance, pensions,
office staff, and other overhead costs. (About £5 at 1982 prices.)

Nature conservation: Maintenance of populations of wild plants
and animals and the natural features on which they depend.

Recreation: Walking, camping, running, or picnicking (within the woodland area).

Softwoods: Coniferous trees, or their timber.

Timber extraction: Moving felled timber from stump to roadside.

APPENDIX 1
Valuation of woodlands for amenity purposes

In 1966 the Author put together some ideas on placing amenity values on trees and woodlands. These were published in August 1967 in the *Journal of the Arboricultural Association*, including suggested systems for arriving at a notional monetary value. The system relating to trees was, with slight modification, adopted by the Tree Council in 1974 and formed the basis of their leaflet *An Evaluation Method for Amenity Trees*. This has been used, with apparently satisfactory results, in a large number of instances, and has enabled a value to be placed on a tree in order to calculate compensation or the amount of money that it might be worth spending in order to ensure the retention of a tree.

The need for a method applicable to woodlands rather than individual trees is no less strong. In particular, there is a need to calculate the relative importance of amenity, compared with timber production, costs of planting, and so on, in any particular woodland, in order to decide whether or not grants should be given for the management of woodland (and, if so, at what level), and to rationalize decision-taking when deciding on the making of Tree Preservation Orders.

The system for valuing woodlands published in 1967 was based on seven factors:

   i. visible area;
   ii. position in the landscape;
  iii. numbers of people in the area;
  iv. presence of other trees and woods;
   v. accessibility;
  vi. condition and type of woodland;
 vii. special values.

This could be altered to include a factor relating to the shape and character of the woodland in relation to the surrounding landscape.

Revising the earlier system, one might have something like this:

FACTOR	UNITS			
	1	2	3	4
i. *Visible area* (ha)	¼ – 1	1 – 5	5 – 20	20 – 100
ii. *Position in landscape*	secluded	average	prominent	very prominent
iii. *Viewing population* (taken as 1% of resident population; plus 1 person per vehicle on roads; plus total population on footpaths or picnic sites)	0 – 1 Remote areas	1 – 20	20 – 100	100+ Populous or popular areas
iv. *Presence of other trees and woods*	Landscape 20 – 50% wooded	Landscape 5 – 20% wooded	Landscape 1 – 5% wooded	Landscape less than 1% wooded
v. *Condition of the woodland*	Young plantations; and blatantly derelict woodlands	Mixed even-aged pole-stage crops	Semi-mature or irregular woodland with fairly large trees	Mature or irregular woodland with very large trees
vi. *Compatibility with the surrounding landscape*	Woodland acceptable in the landscape, but would be considerably improved by change of shape, size, position, or species composition	←	→	Shape, size, position and species composition fully appropriate to the landscape
vii. *Special factors* (Accessibility; well-known beauty spots; screening eyesores)	No special factors	One	Two	Three

The unit scores for each factor are to be multiplied together to give a score for the woodland. This score may then be converted to a notional monetary value by multiplying it by an agreed conversion factor. (£5 per unit score is suggested.) Scores of 0.5, 1.5, and so on, may be used if necessary where a woodland lies between or beyond the suggested sizes, woodland cover percentages, and so forth.

More detailed definitions or descriptions of each factor could be given, as in the Amenity Tree leaflet.

APPENDIX 2
Some typical costs and benefits of managing woodlands of different types (ignoring grants and taxes)
— expressed in man-hour equivalents per hectare per year

1. Size of woodland: 1 ha	Clear felling, spruce	Clear felling, spruce/oak	Group felling spruce/ash	Selection system, Douglas fir /beech
Planting and weeding	3	3	6	3
Fence maintenance	14	13	16	16
Marking and measuring trees	2	1.5	2	3.5
Sale of timber	3	2.5	5	5
Yield control and keeping accounts	0.4	0.4	0.8	0.8
Fire prevention	—	—	—	—
Pest control	—	—	—	—
Brashing and cleaning	1.2	1.2	1.2	1.2
Pruning	0.6	0.3	0.3	0.4
Road maintenance	—	—	—	—
Felling timber	12	7	10	11
Extracting and loading timber	20	13	15	16
Rental	5	5	6	6
Total annual cost per ha	61.2	46.9	62.3	62.9
Annual income per ha from sales of timber, free-on-lorry	40	40	50	45
Amenity value	2	3	4.5	6
Nature conservation value	1	2	3.0	4
Total annual benefit	43	45	57.5	55
Net benefit	−18.2	−1.9	−4.8	−7.9
Ratio of costs : benefits	1:0.70	1:0.96	1:0.92	1:0.87

2. Size of woodland: 10 ha	Clear felling, spruce	Clear felling, spruce/oak	Group felling, spruce/ash	Selection system, Douglas fir /beech
Planting and weeding	2.0	2.0	4.0	2.0
Fence maintenance	4.0	3.6	4.5	4.5
Marking and measuring trees	1.5	1.2	1.5	3.0
Sale of timber	1.0	0.8	1.5	1.6
Yield control and keeping accounts	0.2	0.2	0.4	0.4
Fire prevention	1.0	1.0	0.5	0.5
Pest control	0.1	—	—	1.0
Brashing and cleaning	1.0	1.0	1.0	1.0
Pruning	—	0.1	0.3	0.4
Road maintenance	3.0	3.0	3.0	3.0
Felling timber	9.0	5.0	6.5	7.0
Extracting and loading timber	12.5	7.0	10.0	10.5
Rental	5.0	5.0	6.0	6.0
Total annual cost per ha	40.3	29.9	39.2	40.9
Annual income per ha from sales of timber, free-on-lorry	60	60	65	55
Amenity value	0.7	1.5	3.0	3.5
Nature conservation value	1.0	2.0	3.0	4.0
Total annual benefit	61.5	63.5	71	62.5
Net benefit	21.2	33.6	31.8	21.6
Ratio of costs : benefits	1:1.5	1:2.1	1:1.8	1:1.5

3. Size of woodland: 100 ha	Clear felling, spruce (10 ha coupes)	Clear felling, spruce/oak (10 ha coupes)	Group felling spruce/ash (¼ ha coupes)	Selection system, Douglas fir/ Scots pine
Planting and weeding	2.0	2.0	3.8	1.8
Fence maintenance	1.5	1.6	1.6	1.6
Marking and measuring trees	0.9	0.7	1.2	1.4
Sale of timber	0.5	0.4	0.7	0.8
Yield control and keeping accounts	0.2	0.2	0.6	0.7
Fire prevention	1.0	1.0	0.5	0.5
Pest control	0.1	0.5	0.5	1.0
Brashing and cleaning	0.9	0.9	0.9	0.9
Pruning	—	0.1	0.2	0.3
Road maintenance	2.5	2.5	2.5	2.5
Felling timber	8.0	4.5	5.5	6.0
Extracting and loading timber	10.0	5.5	8.5	9.0
Rental	5.0	5.0	6.0	6.0
Total annual cost per ha	32.6	24.9	32.5	32.5
Annual income per ha from sales of timber, free-on-lorry	70	66	80	70
Amenity value	0.1	0.2	0.4	0.4
Nature conservation value	1	2	3	4
Total annual benefit	71.1	68.2	83.4	74.4
Net benefit	38.5	43.3	50.9	41.9
Ratio of costs : benefits	1:2.2	1:2.7	1:2.6	1:2.3

4. Size of woodland: 1000 ha	Clear felling, spruce and pine (20ha coupes)	Clear felling, spruce/oak/ pine (20ha coupes)	Group felling spruce/ash/ oak/pine	Selection system, Douglas fir/ beech/Scots pine/oak
Planting and weeding	1.9	1.9	3.6	1.6
Fence maintenance	0.6	0.6	0.6	0.6
Marking and measuring trees	0.8	0.6	1.2	1.4
Sale of timber	0.2	0.2	0.4	0.4
Yield control and keeping accounts	0.1	0.1	0.2	0.2
Fire prevention	1.0	1.0	0.2	0.2
Pest control	0.1	0.8	0.8	1.0
Brashing and cleaning	0.8	0.8	0.8	0.8
Pruning	0.4	0.2	0.2	0.3
Road maintenance	2.3	2.3	2.3	2.3
Felling timber	8.0	5.0	5.5	6.0
Extracting and loading timber	8.0	5.0	7.0	7.5
Rental	5.0	5.0	6.0	6.0
Total annual cost per ha	29.2	23.5	28.8	28.3
Annual income per ha from sales of timber, free-on-lorry	75	70	85	75
Amenity value	0.1	0.2	0.3	0.4
Nature conservation value	1	2	3	4
Total annual benefit	76.1	72.2	88.3	79.4
Net benefit	46.9	48.7	59.5	51.1
Ratio of costs : benefits	1:2.6	1:3.1	1:3.1	1:2.8

Clear felling, spruce and pine

	1	2	3	4
5. Size of woodland: 1000ha	*Infertile site at high elevation*	*Fertile site at high elevation liable to early windthrow*	*Infertile site at low elevation*	*Fertile site not liable to early windthrow*
Fertilizing	1.0	0.2	1.0	—
Planting and weeding	1.5	2.5	1.7	2.0
Fencing	0.6	0.6	0.6	0.6
Marking and measuring trees	0.4	0.7	0.6	1.0
Sale of timber	0.2	0.5	0.2	0.3
Yield control and keeping accounts	0.1	0.3	0.1	0.2
Fire prevention	1.0	1.0	1.0	1.0
Pest control	0.1	0.2	0.1	0.1
Brashing and cleaning	0.3	0.6	0.6	1.0
Pruning	—	—	0.4	0.6
Road maintenance	2.0	2.5	1.5	2.0
Felling timber	5.0	9.0	7.0	12.0
Extracting and loading timber	6.0	10.0	7.0	12.0
Rental	4.0	10.0	5.0	7.0
Total annual cost per ha	22.2	38.1	26.8	39.8
Annual income from sales of timber, free-on-lorry	22	52	50	100
Amenity value	2	0.2	2	0.5
Nature conservation value	1	1	2	2
Total annual benefits	25	53.2	54	102.5
Net benefit	2.8	15.1	27.2	62.7
Ratio of costs : benefits	1:1.1	1:1.4	1:2	1:2.6

NOTES